Above The fourteenth century dovecote at
Harlestone.

Following page Northamptonshire in summer:
open farming countryside near Lamport on the
edge of the Northamptonshire Heights.

NORTHAMPTONSHIRE

A PORTRAIT IN COLOUR

TONY NOBLE

Photographs by
John Roan, Paul Martin, Patrick Leonard

THE DOVECOTE PRESS

Cottages in Titchmarsh: the village stands on a ridge above the Nene Valley.

First published in 1995 by The Dovecote Press Ltd
Stanbridge, Wimborne, Dorset BH21 4JD

ISBN 1 874336 36 9

Photographs © John Roan, Paul Martin, Patrick Leonard 1995
Text © Tony Noble 1995

Designed and produced by The Dovecote Press Ltd
Photoset in Sabon by The Typesetting Bureau, Wimborne, Dorset
Printed and bound in Singapore

British Library Cataloguing-in-Publication Data
A Catalogue record of this book is
available from the British Library

1 3 5 7 9 10 8 6 4 2

CONTENTS

NORTHAMPTON 9

STOKE BRUERNE AND TOWCESTER 23

BRACKLEY AND THE SOUTH-WEST 33

DAVENTRY AND THE HEIGHTS 45

ROCKINGHAM FOREST
CORBY AND KETTERING 69

THE NENE VALLEY 95

WELLINGBOROUGH AND THE
SURROUNDING VILLAGES 113

The Photographs 126

Acknowledgements 126

Index 127

NORTHAMPTONSHIRE

LINCOLNSHIRE

LEICESTERSHIRE

R. WELLAND

ROCKINGHAM FOREST

WILLOW BR.

OUNDLE

CORBY

CAMBRIDGE-SHIRE

DESBOROUGH

HARPERS BR.

ROTHWELL

THRAPSTON

KETTERING

BURTON LATIMER

RAUNDS

R. ISE

IRTHLINGBOROUGH

HIGHAM FERRERS

WELLINGBOROUGH

RUSHDEN

WARWICKSHIRE

M45

R. NENE

N

DAVENTRY

NORTHAMPTON HEIGHTS

NORTHAMPTON

BEDFORDSHIRE

TOWCESTER

M1

0   5 MILES   10

R. TOVE

LAND OVER 400 FT.

GRAND UNION CANAL

BRACKLEY

OXFORDSHIRE

R. OUSE

BUCKINGHAMSHIRE

NORTHAMPTONSHIRE

AN old rhyme once described Northamptonshire as being composed of 'mires, squires and spires'. The mires have largely been drained, but one only has to look at the hilltop sites the Saxons chose for many of their villages to realize that the broad Welland and Nene valleys must once have often been flooded. The large number of still lived-in country houses testifies to the survival of many of the squires and their families, whilst the county's church spires are one of its greatest legacies, rising in solid Northamptonshire stone from a landscape patched with villages and small market towns. Improved roads, greater mobility, and a changing agriculture have all had their impact, but the county seems to have escaped the worst excesses of the twentieth century relatively unscathed, still retaining much of its character and charm.

Despite its share of industrial and commercial development Northamptonshire is still a rural county, and there is much that John Clare, the 'peasant poet', would continue to recognize. Clare was born in Helpston near Peterbrough in 1793, but spent most of his often tragic life in Northamptonshire, including over twenty years in the county lunatic asylum in Northampton, where he died in 1864. Clare was a poet of the countryside, and was acutely sensitive to its seasons, forms and colours – perfectly evoking the drowsy heat of high summer in poems like 'Summer Moods':

> *I love to muse o'er meadows newly mown*
> *Where withering grass perfumes the sultry air.*

Northamptonshire's thin elliptical shape is approximately 70 miles long and 25 miles wide at its broadest. It contains several well-defined geographical regions, with the belt of Liassic rock and Oolitic limestone which forms its geological backbone providing the county with a whole range of high quality building stones, many of which can still be seen in its churches and houses. Quarries at King's Cliffe in Rockingham Forest yielded an oolite much used for elaborate carved decoration. Collyweston has long been famous for its roofing slates. The stone for much of King's College Chapel, Cambridge, and both Eleanor Crosses in the county, came from the limestone quarries at Weldon; as did the stone for such houses as Kirby Hall and Castle Ashby.

Northamptonshire is generally regarded as being part of the great Midland plain, and only a handful of its hills reach the 400 feet contour. But the scarp and slopes of the Heights form the watershed for a whole range of river systems, and few places are more than a mile or two from water. The Cherwell, Tove and Great Ouse are formed on the southern slopes of the Northamptonshire Heights. The River Avon rises near Naseby, as does the River Welland before meandering north-eastwards into the Wash. The county's biggest river, the Nene, begins life south of Daventry in the steep-sided valleys between Badby and Staverton. It then flows north, passing through Northampton,

Wellingborough, Thrapston and Oundle, and influencing the character of much of the central and eastern side of the county.

It was up rivers like the Welland and Nene that the first Saxons sailed, later using them to transport building stone for their churches in flat-bottomed barges. Saxon settlements are scattered all along the Nene Valley, usually nestling on south-facing slopes where the rich alluvial soil was most workable. Once again it is John Clare who best describes the tranquil character of rural village life in the county:

The evening gathers from the gloomy woods
And darkling creeps o'er silent vale and hill
While the snug village in nights happy moods
Is resting calm and beautifully still

Northamptonshire's central position has inevitably meant it being washed to and fro by the tides of history. The Romans built a fort alongside their new road of Watling Street at Towcester. Many a Saxon settlement was sacked by the Vikings. The Normans built both Rockingham and Northampton castles. Richard III was born at Fotheringhay Castle in 1452, and it was there that the tragic Mary Queen of Scots ended her days beneath the executioner's axe in 1587. The funeral cortege of Edward I's much-loved queen travelled south through the county in 1290, and the two Eleanor Crosses at Geddington and Hardingstone remain as her memorial. The most decisive battle of the Civil War ended in Cromwell's victory over Charles I at Naseby at 1645.

Amongst those involved in the Civil War were the Arkwrights from Aynho, the Drydens of Canons Ashby and the Knightleys of Fawsley. Such families founded their wealth in the wake of the Dissolution of the Monasteries by Henry VIII, which transferred Northamptonshire's monastic houses into the hands of a new generation of Tudor merchants and gentry. The 7th Earl of Cardigan, who led the Light Brigade into the 'valley of death' at Balaclava, was born a Brudenhall at Deene Park. The Princess of Wales must thank a sixteenth century sheep farmer called John Spencer for her childhood at Althorp House.

Northampton first made boots in 1213 for King John when he was staying at the Castle. By the middle of the nineteenth century they could be found in every corner of the Empire. As the industry expanded, it spread outwards from the county town, providing employment in Wellingborough and Kettering, as well as dozens of 'boot and shoe' villages. Mechanisation and cheap imports have reduced shoe-making to a shadow of its former self, a fate suffered by the steel-making town of Corby – which mushroomed from village to town in twenty years thanks to the ironstone beds on which it stands.

Just as Northamptonshire's position at the heart of England has shaped its past, so also is it helping determine its future. The opening of the M1 motorway in 1959 linked it both to London and the north, attracting new industries. Yet what the superb collection of photographs taken for this book has most reminded me is how essentially rural much of the county still remains. There are landscapes, country houses, villages and towns, the long stretches of canal and river passing through unspoilt countryside, the undulating slopes of the Northamptonshire Heights – all of which combine to provide a portrait of a county that has as much to offer as anywhere in England.

TONY NOBLE
Moulton

NORTHAMPTON

NORTHAMPTON

Northamptonshire's county town sits on the north bank of the River Nene where it is joined by a smaller tributary, called the North Water. The two rivers act as a natural defensive barrier and crossing point, and now provide the town with a park and meadow close to its centre. Northampton's position so close to the middle of England has long made it nationally prominent. The Saxons first settled on the site, probably in about 650 AD, gradually building a town that was later sacked by the Vikings. By the date of the Norman Conquest in 1066 the town had been rebuilt, and the new invaders chose it as both an administrative centre for the Midlands and the site of a traditional motte-and-bailey castle, built where the railway station now stands.

The town plan has changed little since the thirteenth century. Its medieval entrances and gates correspond to the main roads that converge on it today. The line of the now-vanished medieval walls can still be equated to a line including Campbell Square, Lower Mounts, Cheyne Walk, Victoria Promenade, and St Andrew's Road. Undoubtedly, the greatest calamity to befall the town was the Great Fire of 1675, which swept through its heart and destroyed virtually every building in the Market Square, leaving only the Welsh House and the tower of All Saints church. The fire began in the home of a poor woman in St Mary's Street, when the live coals she was carrying in a shovel to cook with were blown onto the thatch. Fanned by a strong west wind, and fuelled by the oil and tallow stores in College Street, nearly half the town had been reduced to embers by the time the fire burnt itself out. Despite such disasters, Northampton, through its people and buildings, remains a town rich in character. The Church of the Holy Sepulchre, close to the original medieval north gate, is probably its oldest building, dating from 1100, and is the best preserved of the four remaining round churches in the country.

The town has a distinguished past. It received its Charter from Richard I in 1189 and during the thirteenth century the Castle was the meeting place for the English Parliament. It was here that Thomas a Becket was put on trial by Henry II in 1164, and in 1215 the Castle was besieged for a fortnight during an uprising against King John. Through much of the medieval period the town boasted a school the equal of Oxford, and which might easily have blossomed into a great university had not its students sided with Simon de Montfort in his revolt against Henry III. Yet Northampton remains better known for its part in the struggles between king and parliament than as a place of learning. Henry VI defeated Edward, Earl of March, at the Battle of Northampton in 1460 – an important conflict in The Wars of the Roses. Soon after the Civil War, Charles II ordered the destruction of the Castle and town walls.

Its days of glory apparently over, Northampton was saved from obscurity by the least likely of its traditional industries – boot and shoe-making. Both had been made in the town for centuries, indeed Cromwell's Roundhead army marched to Naseby shod in

Previous page Fireworks burst high over Abington Park Lake on the final Saturday of the Northampton Summer Show, which is held in mid-July and traditionally ends in this explosion of colour and noise.

Northampton boots, but the arrival of the Industrial Revolution revived Northampton's fortunes, spawning a dictionary of words and phrases associated with the trade: 'clickers', 'closers', and the 'rough stuff men'. The red-brick terraces marched outwards, absorbing such villages as Abington as the town expanded. The industry reached its height at the end of the nineteenth century. But shoe-making is now a thing of the past, commemorated by the 'Cobbler's Last' statue in Abington Street. In recent years the old factories have been taken over by newer industries trading on the town's geographical position. Yet there is much in Northampton to enjoy, and the presence of its parks and rivers give it a rural character that continues to bear-out Daniel Defoe's description of it in the 1720s as 'the handsomest and best built town in all this part of England'.

Above 'The Cobbler's Last', the 12 feet high bronze statue by Graham Ibbestone which has stood in the centre of Abington Street since 1986 as a symbol of the industry that brought the town its wealth. A 'last' was originally a wooden model of the foot, on which shoemakers shaped and repaired boots and shoes. The two children are intended to symbolize the regeneration of the town in the 1960s.

Right The canvas sea covering Northampton's famous Market Square. The Square is reputed to be the second largest in England – after Nottingham – and has been a bustling centre of trade since 1235, when Henry III ordered that the selling of goods next door in All Saints churchyard should stop and move to a new position in the Square. The two hundred or so stalls are surrounded on all sides by a mixture of Georgian and Victorian buildings alongside several modern shopping developments.

Behind the apples on sale in the foreground stands the Welsh House, which thanks to being built of stone was the only building in the Market Square to survive the ravages of the Great Northampton Fire in 1675. The site was bought in 1594 for £80 by an Anglesey lawyer and former rector of Maidwell and Castle Ashby, Dr William Prytherch, who built the house a year later. The building was restored in 1975 and given a new coat of arms with its original Welsh motto, 'HEB DYW HEB DYM DYW A DIGON', meaning 'WITHOUT GOD, WITHOUT ANYTHING; [WITH] GOD AND ENOUGH'. The original building also featured the initials WEP, which are included in the new facade and commemorate William Prytherch and the first of his three wives, Elizabeth. The four shields facing out over the Market Square represent the Welsh dragon, the Wake family of Courteenhall, the arms of William Prytherch, and those of an unknown family. The house is possibly a relic of the days when Welsh drovers brought their cattle down through the Midlands to markets in Northampton and Banbury.

Beethoven House with its superb Gothic oriel window overlooks the lively Market Square. The seventeenth century building owes its name to the music school founded in it in 1886 by Brook Sampson, the organist at nearby All Saints Church. Since then it has been used as a Ladies School, by the War Office, as a study centre, and solicitors' offices.

The centre of Northampton looking towards The Drapery – a street lined with a range of eighteenth and nineteenth century buildings and originally named after the many drapers who occupied the west side from the fourteenth century onwards. The east side was once called The Glovery, after the glovers who worked there.

The Sessions House in George Row, built immediately after the Great Fire of 1675 and which stands between the former County Hall and the Judge's Lodgings. The Quarter Sessions used to be held in the town Castle, but because Northampton supported Parliament during the Civil War Charles II had it burnt to the ground in 1662, shortly after the Restoration. The courtrooms inside the Sessions House have a magnificent though divided plaster ceiling designed by Edward Goudge between 1684 and 1688: included in the decorations is a devil whose tongue is reputed to wag if witnesses in the court below tell a lie!

Above The Public Library, Abington Street. The statue over the door is of John Dryden (1631-1700), Northamptonshire's Poet Laureate. On the opposite side is a statue of Thomas Fuller (1608-1661), another poet, and in the centre are the busts of Lawrence Washington, the builder of Sulgrave Manor, and Andrew Carnegie, the Scottish-born philanthropist and steel magnate who gave the money for the building of the library in 1910.

Above & left Northampton Town Hall, a rich architectural conception whose facade of statues, shields and sculptured scenes unfolds like a history in stone of both the town and county. Built by Edward Godwin in the 1860's out of Northamptonshire stone, its lavish Victorian Gothic design incorporates the Great Fire (1675), the Battle of Northampton (1460), Thomas a Becket's trial in Northampton Castle (1164) and the execution of Mary Queen of Scots (1587). Below the ground floor windows are fifty shields representing villages, towns, trades, crafts and notable local families. Inside, in the Great Hall, a series of paintings echo the same historical themes, including one of the town's possible founder, Alfred the Great.

The photograph on the left is a closer view of part of the facade. Fourteen statues stand beneath canopies between the first-floor windows, and the five shown here (from left to right) are: Henry III (1216-1272), who attempted to found a university in the town and was a regular visitor to the Castle; Edward I (1272-1307), who ordered the building of the Eleanor Crosses (of which two of the three survivors stand in Northamptonshire) in memory of his queen; Queen Victoria (1837-1901), who visited the town in 1844; Henry VIII (1509-1547), who by dissolving the monasteries allowed their estates to be acquired by the county's 'squires'; and Edward IV (1461-1483), who defeated Henry VI at the Battle of Northampton in 1460 and later married Elizabeth Woodville at Grafton Regis. The other nine are of Saint Michael (Northampton's patron saint); Saints George, Patrick and Andrew; Thomas a Becket; Queen Eleanor; Sir Thomas White, a town benefactor; the poet John Dryden; and Richard I, who granted the town its charter in 1189.

The traditional Oak Apple Day procession on May 29th, which commemorates Charles II's triumphal return into London after the Restoration of 1660. Charles II's affection for Northampton seems to have veered from one extreme to the other. Thirteen years after ordering the destruction of the Castle, he gave a thousand tons of oak from Whittlewood Forest to help restore the church after the Great Fire of 1675.

Placing an oak wreath during the Oak Apple Day ceremony on the statue of Charles II, dressed in a Roman tunic, which adorns the centre of the balustrade on the portico of All Saints Church. The only Norman stonework to survive the Great Fire are the four large pillars supporting the tower. It was under the shadow of the portico that John Clare (1793-1864), the county's peasant poet, spent hours watching the world drift by after wandering there from the asylum where he was a patient, a pathetic and forlorn figure.

St Crispin's Street Fayre, held in the town centre for the first time during October 1994 to celebrate the birthday on October 25th of the Patron Saint of Shoemakers.

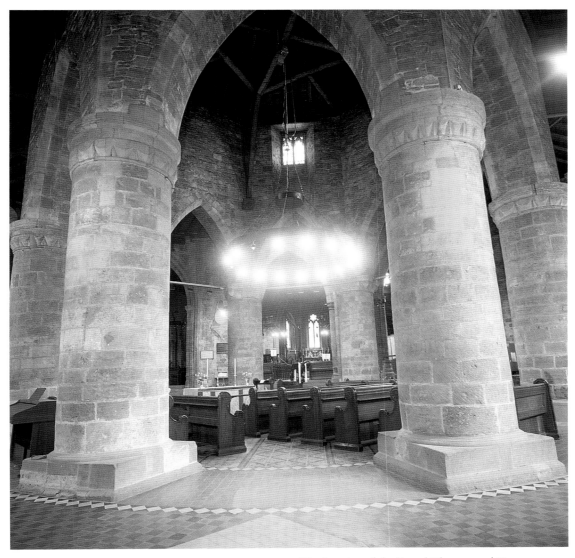

The Church of the Holy Sepulchre, built by Simon de Senlis, Earl of Northampton, in 1099 as a thanksgiving and offering for his safe return from the Crusades (he died a few years later returning from a second Crusade). It is now one of only four round churches left in England and is probably the largest and best preserved and most like the original in Jerusalem. Immediately on entering the church you step down into the 'round' and become surrounded by eight massive circular Norman pillars. The building was the garrison church of the former Northamptonshire Regiment and contains a large number of military memorials. Near the door and just above head height is a Saxon mass dial showing the time of the services, and which is thought to stand on the site of the former church.

The interior of the Royal Theatre and Opera House, designed by the famous theatrical designer Charles Phipps, who also built the Savoy Theatre in London. The building opened in 1884, and was promptly restored following a disastrous fire three years later. A fine example of Baroque Victorian architecture, complete with private boxes supported on Corinthian pillars, it has a wonderful safety curtain painted by Henry Bird in the 1970s showing the 'ages of man'. Look particularly for the shadowy figures moving across the bottom, which start on the left with a baby held aloft, and end on the right with an old man bent over a walking stick.

Above An assortment of rafts passing Midsummer Meadow during the annual Raft Race held in the summer on the River Nene in Northampton. Companies and groups of individuals build their own rafts and compete as a way of raising money for charity. The race is essentially light-hearted and, having taken part, I know that good weather and a raft that floats are essential to avoid a ducking.

Right 'Going, going, gone.' Sheep being sold at Northampton's cattle market, which is soon to move from Victoria Promenade to a new site at Brackmills.

Below The Church of St Peter and St Paul, Abington, which stands beside the Manor House, now a museum, in a delightful position on the edge of town on the road through Abington Park. The landscaped 100 acre park is one of Northampton's largest, and contains flower gardens, lakes, rare trees, aviaries and play areas.

Bottom right Other than the Castle Mound in the corner of the Chalk Lane car park, all that is left of Northampton Castle is the Postern Gate near the entrance to the Railway Station. Originally a Norman 'motte and bailey' castle built in 1084 by Simon de Senlis, and later strengthened, the castle's fortunes declined during the fourteenth century. Its days finally ended in 1662 when Charles II ordered its destruction to avenge the support given to Cromwell by the town during the Civil War.

Right Becket's Well, on the Bedford Road leading out of town, remains the only memorial to the flight of Thomas à Becket disguised as a monk following his trial at Northampton Castle in 1164. The close friendship between Becket and Henry II had soured once Becket became Archbishop of Canterbury, and in October 1164 he was brought to trial accused of inefficiency during his period as Chancellor. The charges were unimportant, and in reality were no more than a pretext by which Henry intended to bring about the complete ruin of his former favourite. One night, after celebrating mass at St Andrew's Priory, Becket slipped out of town on his way into exile in France, supposedly pausing to drink from the well. His reprieve was brief. Two years later he was murdered in Canterbury Cathedral, where his tomb remains a place of pilgrimage to this day.

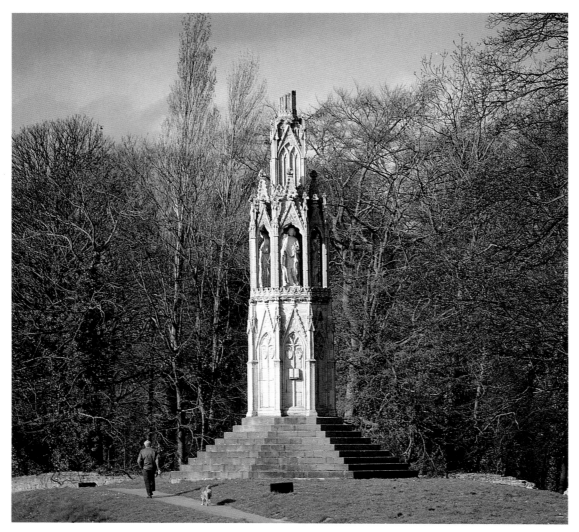

The Queen Eleanor Cross, Hardingstone, near Delapre Park on the London Road out of Northampton. It was here at Delapre Abbey that the coffin and cortege of Queen Eleanor rested for the night on the way to Westminster Abbey following her death in Nottinghamshire in 1290. After her burial, Edward I ordered that each of the twelve overnight stops made by the funeral procession during the 150 mile journey should be marked wiith an 'Eleanor Cross' in memory of his queen. Only three remain, at Hardingstone and Geddington in Northamptonshire, and Waltham Cross in Hertfordshire. Although the top of the Hardingstone Cross is missing, the second stage contains four statues of the queen facing each of the compass points.

Reaching for the ball during a line-out at Northampton Rugby Club. 'The Saints' were founded in 1880 by the Reverend Samuel Wigg, the curate of St James' Church, and are now one of the premier clubs in the country. Originally called Northampton St James, the club was started as a youth club to enable a few high spirited lads to channel their energies and to bring law and order to the parish! In 1886 a local pleasure garden on the Weedon Road was purchased by John Franklin, a successful hotelier, renamed Franklin's Gardens, and it has been the home of 'The Saints' ever since. Over the years the Club has discovered and developed some of the greatest players to wear an international Rugby shirt. It remains as popular as ever, arousing intense passion and loyalty throughout the town.

A championship match in progress between Northamptonshire and Surrey at the County Cricket Ground, Abington Avenue, Northampton. The first recorded mention of cricket being played in the county dates to 1741 when 'Eleven Gentlemen of Northamptonshire' took to the field. Although there was a cricket club in the town as early as 1775, the present County Club grew naturally out of the Northampton Town Club formed in 1878. The county side played its first match on the present ground eight years later, losing to Surrey Club and Ground by six wickets.

The smaller photograph shows Northampton-shire's captain since 1989, Allan Lamb, in a characteristic pose. Lamb was born in South Africa in 1954, and made his county debut in 1978, winning his county cap that season. He first played for England four years later, and was a regular member of the team for almost a decade, playing in over 50 tests. Cricketing connoisseurs regard Lamb's attacking approach to batting as his greatest asset and a tribute to his vast experience in one day games, both at County and International level.

Northampton at work viewed from the top of the Express Lift Tower, affectionately known to locals as the 'Lighthouse'. In the centre are the towers of the Carlsberg Brewery, opened in 1974 by Princess Benedikte of Denmark on the site of a previous brewery. In the background, where open fields and rural Northamptonshire begin to appear, is the Brackmills Industrial Estate, which has developed since the beginning of the 1980s.

STOKE BRUERNE AND TOWCESTER

STOKE BRUERNE AND TOWCESTER

NEARLY two thousand years ago Watling Street echoed to the tramp of the Roman legions marching north from London to Chester and their military posts in North Wales. Towcester was then a fort called *Lactodorum*, and a key staging-post, but although still divided by Watling Street it now sits quietly beside its bypass. Following the departure of the Romans both the Saxons and Normans continued to develop the town, building its first church and strengthening its walls.

Just as Watling Street sparked Towcester's original development, so also did it transform the medieval town and initiate its period of greatest prosperity. During the coaching era Towcester bustled with coaches making the long journey north to Holyhead and the Irish ferries. The peak was reached in the 1830s. Charles Dickens was a frequent visitor to the Saracen's Head Hotel, which he immortalized as the Pomfret Arms in *The Pickwick Papers* as the scene of the election argument between Pott and Shirk.

If Towcester owes its rise to a road, then Stoke Bruerne can equally be said to be the

Previous page Traditional canal art and craft alongside the towpath of the Grand Union Canal at Stoke Bruerne.

An aerial view, which although only taken a few miles from the centre of Northampton, gives a good idea of the typically rural countryside that fills much of the south of the county. The church in the background is St John the Baptist, Piddington. In the foreground is part of Hackleton, which clings to the old turnpike road to Stoke Goldington. The two villages perfectly sum up the impact of roads on small communities. Hackleton has no church and was once only a hamlet, but the arrival of the turnpike in 1709, which bypassed Piddington, helped Hackleton expand at Piddington's expense.

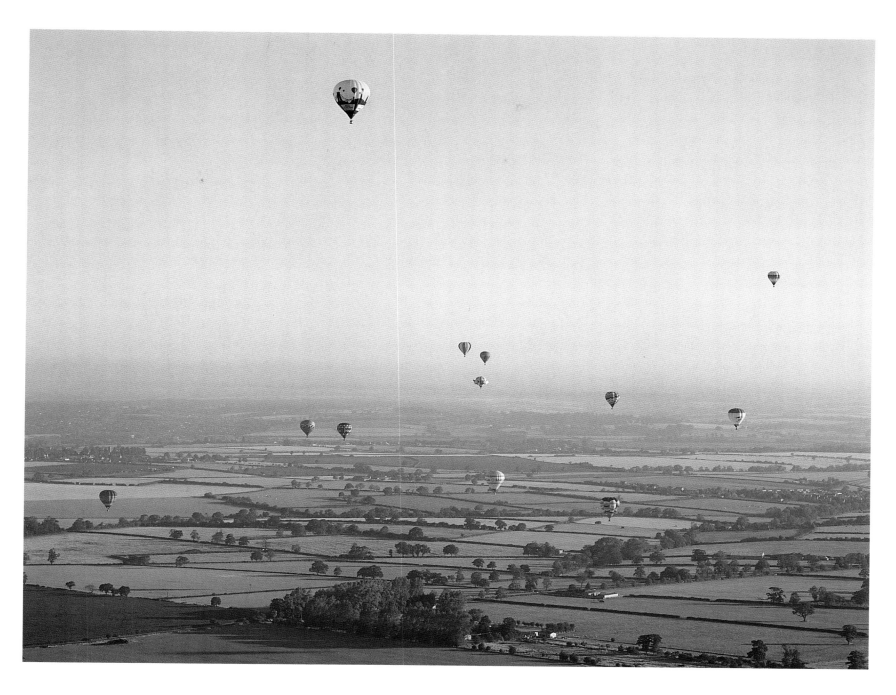

Hot air balloons soar high over the open slightly wooded countryside between Hackleton and Salcey Forest after taking off from the old Race Course during Northampton's annual August Balloon Festival.

child of a canal. What is now the Grand Union Canal originally opened in 1805 as the Grand Junction Canal linking London to Birmingham. For nearly half a century bargees and boatmen unhitched their horses at the entrance to the Blisworth Tunnel in readiness for the unenviable task of 'legging' it the length of the 3056 yard long tunnel. As well as joining London to the Midlands markets, the Grand Union brought a whole range of cheaper goods into Northamptonshire – pottery, coal, lime and fertiliser – as well as enabling it to transport local produce to towns on or near the canal. The history of the canal is as evocative as any, and is today well-served by the Canal Museum at Stoke Bruerne, converted from an old corn mill.

Narrowboats moored between Stoke Bruerne and the Blisworth Tunnel, a five minute walk along the towpath from the Canal Museum. By 1790 a national canal network had been established linking the Mersey, Humber, Severn and Thames; but there was no direct link between Birmingham and the Thames. In 1792 a scheme was put forward for a Grand Junction Canal linking the Oxford Canal at Braunston to London, and building began a year later. Geological problems at Blisworth defeated two attempts to tunnel beneath the hill, and finally a a suggested flight of locks was rejected in favour of a 'plateway' for horse-drawn wagons connecting the two sections. The Grand Junction Canal opened in 1799, and for the next six years cargoes from Birmingham and London were unloaded at Blisworth and Stoke Bruerne and carried by wagons along the 'plateway', then reloaded. The 3056 yard long Blisworth Tunnel finally opened in 1805, and remains the longest navigable tunnel in Britain. Near the entrance is a brick hut, built originally as a shelter for 'leggers', men who lay on top of the narrow boats and 'walked' the entire length of the tunnel sides or roof.

The Grand Union Canal at Stoke Bruerne. A restored corn mill is now the Canal Museum. Containing photographs, maps, documents, clothing, models and the arts and crafts associated with the Grand Union, it illustrates life on the canal in a fresh and lively way. The picturesque setting is enhanced by boats negotiating the locks against the background of the pack-horse bridge.

Temple House, or New Temple, Horton, was built as one of a series of buildings by Lord Halifax in the eighteenth century to act as 'eyecatchers' from the now demolished Horton Hall. Lord Halifax was financially ruined after supporting an unsuccessful candidate in Parliamentary elections in 1768. The rumbustious three-corned fight was between candidates supported by the Earls Halifax, Northampton and Spencer of Horton, Castle Ashby and Althorp respectively. Despite the expenditure of £160,000 the vote was tied, and the election decided on the toss of a coin. Lord Halifax was ruined by his losses, and his estate was forfeited to the government. Horton Hall was finally demolished in the 1930s, but Temple House and a triumphal arch still stand.

Opposite page The River Ouse at Cosgrove follows the Northamptonshire and Buckinghamshire border for several miles.

Right The 'Iron Trunk' aqueduct which spans the River Ouse at Cosgrove and links Northamptonshire with Buckinghamshire. Several attempts were made to cross the Ouse Valley, first by a series of locks and then by aqueduct – at least one of which collapsed. The 'Iron Trunk' finally opened in 1811, and is today cared for by English Heritage. To reach it from Cosgrove walk down from the Barley Mow Inn and under the canal footpath tunnel, continuing along the towpath to the right for about half a mile.

Watling Street, Towcester, reputedly the oldest town in Northamptonshire. The Romans called it *Lactodorum* and fortified it during the first century. The site of the southern Roman gateway is thought to have spanned Watling Street at Richmond Road, further down the road from the Town Hall. During the Saxon period in the early tenth century Edward the Elder continued to develop the town, strengthening its walls and building St Laurence's Church. In the Civil War Towcester was occupied by Prince Rupert for the Royalists, and in the nineteenth century it became a busy staging post on the main route north from London. In the foreground is the brick-built Post Office, a fine Georgian building dating to 1799.

Left The fifteenth century Chantry House at Towcester stands next to the Post Office and was formerly the old Grammar School, founded by William Sponne in his will, rector from 1422 to 1448 and a great benefactor to the town (his effigy, complete with gruesome skeleton, can be seen in the church). The house served as a school and master's residence until 1866, since when it has largely been rebuilt – although the fifteenth century gate arch still stands.

Below A thatcher at work on a cottage in Alderton, a village just off the A5 near Towcester. Northamptonshire is blessed with a great deal of thatch, and happily it is still not unusual to see craftsmen at work on its roofs.

The glorious gate screen built in 1822 as an approach to Easton Neston Manor, the home of Lord Hesketh. The gates, complete with urns adorning the screens and deer on the end lodges, now mark the entrance to Towcester Races. The original village of Easton Neston was gradually abandoned when the Manor was enclosed by a park in the sixteenth century, and the land changed from arable to pasture. Such changes were not uncommon where a large manorial house dominated the village in its shadow, and the same fate befell Fawsley, where the tenants were forced from their cottages as their fields were transformed into grazing for sheep.

Horses and jockeys taking a jump during a meeting at Towcester Races, held on several occasions during the year and a popular gathering-place for the local racing fraternity.

BRACKLEY AND THE SOUTH-WEST

BRACKLEY AND THE
SOUTH-WEST

THE open rural countryside between Daventry and Brackley enables the traveller to explore a feast of superbly picturesque scenery, whose skyline is occasionally broken by small hamlets, which often nestle together around a ridge or stream. The Northamptonshire Heights extend south towards Brackley, providing the source of several rivers – the Nene, Tove and Ouse. Parts of the county's south-western border are fringed by the River Cherwell and the Oxford Canal. There is more than a hint of the Cotswolds in the stone of many of the villages, and the countryside round Kings Sutton and Aynho, whose fruit-covered walls are a reminder of the time when its lord of the manor requested payment in apricots, is as glorious as anywhere in the county. The only noise to shatter the peace comes from the famous international circuit at Silverstone, once an airfield, where there is now motor-racing on many weekends.

Northamptonshire is rich in buildings, towns and villages with an American connection. Perhaps the best known is Sulgrave Manor, north-west of Brackley and the home of the Washington family between 1539 and 1656. For many the Manor is a place of pilgrimage whose gardens and period rooms give a real flavour of the world into which the ancestors of the first President of the United States, George Washington, were born.

Further north is Canons Ashby, another of Northamptonshire's great houses, and once the home of the Dryden family. John Dryden (1631-1700), a descendant, was appointed the Poet Laureate in 1670 and visited the house frequently in the 1650's. Only the fish-ponds of its priory survive, whilst the thirteenth century church is unique in being only one of a handful left in the country still in the gift of the lord of the manor. During the late eighteenth century the area was the haunt of the notorious Culworth Gang, a group of highwaymen whose depredations included holding-up coaches, robbing travellers and pillaging homes. Many of its members were known, but so fearful were the locals of falling foul of them that no one risked betraying them. Even the parish clerk of Sulgrave played his part, helping hide much of their loot in the church. They were eventually caught breaking into a house near Blakesley, and four ended their days in the hangman's noose at Northampton in 1787.

Names like Hinton-in-the-Hedges, Snorscomb, and Moreton Pinkney call the roll on villages that still retain an essentially rural character. Just as they seem to grow naturally out of the surrounding landscape, so also does the area's only town. Brackley's spacious tree-lined main street is over a mile long, and its mixture of brick and stone buildings lend the whole town considerable historical charm. Several belong to Magdalen College School, whilst the Town Hall given to Brackley by the Duke of Bridgewater in 1706 dominates the Market Place.

Previous page Sun and shadow in a quiet lane in Aynho, a hillside village overlooking the edge of the Cotswolds in the southern corner of the county.

A bird's-eye view of the 1994 British Grand Prix at Silverstone Race Circuit. Originally an airfield used for training Royal Air Force bomber pilots during the Second World War, its runways remained deserted until 1948, when tents, pits, scaffolding frames and rope barriers appeared as the Royal Automobile Club prepared for the post-war return of Grand Prix Racing. The 1948 Grand Prix was won by Luigi Villoresi driving a Maserati at a speed of 72 mph round a track marked with oil drums and straw bales. Today Silverstone is a sophisticated sports centre and business complex, but it remains best known for the Formula 1 British Grand Prix. Throughout the year the track is in constant demand for testing, racing and skid school tuition, as well as the traditional racing weekends – which can include motor cycles, trucks and vintage cars.

The smaller photograph shows Damon Hill leading the field into the first bend during the 1994 British Grand Prix.

The first bluebells coming into flower in the south of the county near Syresham. The most characteristic feature of Northamptonshire's eighteenth century landscape was its openness, but by the mid-nineteenth century the impact of enclosure had affected half the county. The area round Syresham was not immune, and the hedges that so delight us today were largely planted to mark boundaries and create a pattern of much smaller fields.

Brackley High Street. The spacious tree-lined main street is over a mile long, and the old brick and stone buildings that line it give the town a sense of provincial charm. Roman coins and pottery found in the district suggest that there was a Roman settlement at Brackley, but the Middle Ages marked its heyday. The wool trade brought wealth, and a Castle (which no longer stands), as well as the Hospital of St James and St John – now the School chapel and chapel-of-ease to the parish church. By the eighteenth century Brackley was in decline and well-known locally for the vagabonds and rogues who took refuge in the town – hence the couplet:

Brackley bred.
Better to hang than to feed.

Above Brackley School. The exact date of the school's sixteenth century foundation is uncertain, but its reputation was sufficiently high by 1556 for Trinity College, Oxford, to name it as one of the schools – together with Eton, Reading and Banbury – from which scholars were to be recruited. In 1860 the school expanded to become a thriving Grammar School, and the original buildings have since been absorbed into the town's comprehensive school.

Left Brackley Town Hall, a fine building dominating the south end of the High Street. Originally erected on arches in 1706 by the 1st Duke of Bridgewater at a cost of £2000, it initially provided a covered market area. In 1884 it became a Corn Exchange and the lower storey arches were enclosed.

An unusual dovecote built into the gable wall of a thatched cottage in Blacksmith's Hill, Aynho.

Aynhoe Hall, now a rest home, which stands in Aynhoe Park on the edge of the village. The Hall and estate were acquired in 1615 by Richard Cartwright, who deliberately added the 'e'. The original house was burnt down by defeated Royalists fleeing from Naseby, undoubtedly because its owner, John Cartwright, was well-known for supporting Cromwell. The Hall was rebuilt and extended at the end of the seventeenth century, and after three centuries of ownership the Cartwrights finally sold Aynhoe in 1960.

Right A narrowboat moored beside a bridge over the River Cherwell at Kings Sutton, near where the river and Oxford Canal follow the county boundary.

Below The medieval church of St Peter and St Paul, Kings Sutton, lies at the heart of the village adjacent to the green. Within the vicinity of the green are the seventeenth century manor and the old sixteenth century court house, now a private dwelling.

Above The 'stars and stripes' flying in the garden of Sulgrave Manor, the home of the ancestors of George Washington (1732-1799), the first President of the United States of America. The Manor was built during the middle of the sixteenth century by Lawrence Washington, who bought the estate from Henry VIII, and his descendants lived there until John Washington emigrated to Virginia in 1656. For the next 250 years the house had several owners, but in 1914 it was given by a group of British subscribers to the people of Great Britain and the United States as a way of celebrating a century of peace between the two countries. The Manor is now open to the public, and there is much to enjoy, including Tudor and Queen Anne furnishings, the eighteenth century kitchen – as well as spring daffodils and summer rose gardens.

Right Canons Ashby, the home of the Dryden family from 1550 until 1981 when the house was donated to the National Trust. Canons Ashby takes its name from the Augustinian canons who built a priory on the site in the twelfth century. The original buildings stood around the church of St Mary Magdalene, which still survives, and which, since the Dissolution of the Monasteries in 1536 has been part of the Canons Ashby Estate. The house is a truly wonderful memorial to the Dryden family, and remains one of the oldest and most romantic of all Northamptonshire's great houses. The painted wall decoration and spectacular plasterwork ceiling in the Great Chamber are complemented by the gardens, with their terraces, stone walls set with vases and the magnificent Baroque gate-piers.

Above The rolling countryside near Culworth, now a tranquil backwater of copses and hedged fields. The area was once notorious for a band of highwaymen, led by John Smith, whose activities only ceased when several members of the gang were caught and executed in Northampton in 1787.

Left A lone rider surrounded by the bright yellow of oilseed rape near Badby.

Above Everdon village nestling in its valley and surrounded by the rolling countryside of the Heights. The village is mentioned in a Saxon charter and at the time of the Domesday Book in 1086 belonged to the Bishop of Bayeaux. It later became the property of the Benedictine Abbey of Bernay in Normandy. The fourteenth century church of St Mary's is large for a village and has one of the finest tracery screens in the country.

Right Charwelton's thirteenth century packhorse bridge spans the infant waters of the River Cherwell, which rises in the village. Charwelton is unusual in that during the Middle Ages it consisted of two villages sharing one church. The church now stands almost isolated at Church Charwelton, with the surviving village clustered around the main Daventry to Banbury road.

Fawsley Hall, the home of the Knightleys for over 500 years. The estate was bought by the family in 1415 and the original hall built in 1540. One member, Sir Richard Knightley, was present at the execution of Mary Queen of Scots at Fotheringay in 1587 and helped bear the canopy at her funeral. For centuries the Knightleys appear to have been plagued by a lack of money, and in 1921 Sir Charles Knightley sold off 22,000 acres in a desperate but short-lived attempt to hang on to the Hall. It was finally sold in 1938, remaining melancholy and deserted until used by a timber company in the 1960s. Happily, Fawsley Hall and its surrounding parkland have since been renovated and restored.

Fawsley Lakes, with St Mary's Church just visible through the trees. The village of Fawsley was abandoned soon after the Knightley's bought the manor and began evicting their tenants to make way for sheep pasture. Its remains lie under the lakes and park created by 'Capability' Brown during the eighteenth century, leaving the village church standing isolated on a hill overlooking the lakes. St Mary's is worth visiting for the many monuments to the Knightley family, and to enjoy what many regard as one of Northamptonshire's most enchanted corners.

DAVENTRY AND
THE HEIGHTS

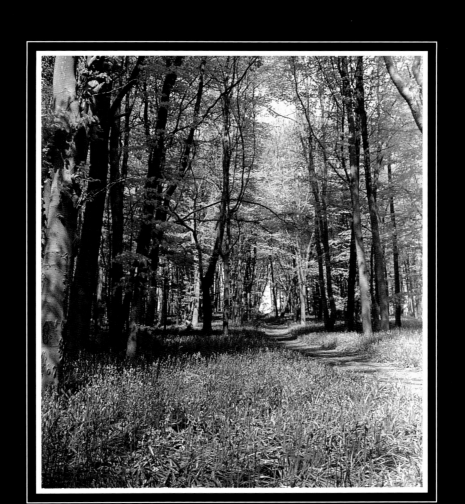

DAVENTRY AND THE HEIGHTS

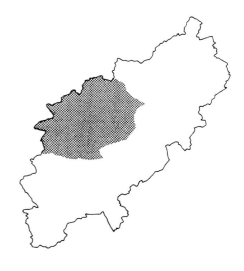

THE gentle weathered hills of the Northamptonshire Heights roll across this area of the county. The Heights are a natural extension of the Cotswolds, unveiling woods, undulating pasture and attractive unspoilt countryside in succession. The scarp and slopes form the watershed for several important river systems. The Avon begins its journey west into the Bristol Channel 600 feet above sea level in a muddle of streams near Naseby. The Welland also rises close by, meandering slowly northwards towards the Wash and forming much of the county's northern border.

The views out over the Welland Valley from the rim of what was once Rockingham Forest are more than matched by those from the Jurassic Way. The Way runs along the limestone Heights, acting as the hub to what were once several prehistoric routeways across the county. On one such route stands Borough Hill, the fortified Iron Age hill-fort on the outskirts of Daventry that was once probably a major tribal centre. Centuries later the Romans built a villa on the site, which looked down towards Watling Street, their great road to the north. In the seventeenth century the Royalist army of Charles I camped on the hill before marching to defeat at Naseby. Later still, when Daventry was known for its whip-making, local sportsmen wagered and raced the horses across its

Previous page The bluebell wood at Coton Manor Gardens, which in spring attracts many visitors. The gardens form a marvellous old English garden, creatively laid out with herbaceous borders, rose and water gardens, and lakes graced by waterfowl and flamingoes.

Ashby St Ledgers, the Tudor home of the ill-starred Catesby family for about 250 years from around 1375. The first Catesby to fall victim to history was William, who as a favourite of Richard III was executed three days after the Battle of Bosworth in 1485: his tomb dates his death to two days before the battle, perhaps to suggest a death by natural causes. The Catesbys sold the manor in 1612, and it was eventually bought in 1903 by the 2nd Lord Wimborne, who employed Lutyens to remodel both the house and gardens.

slopes. Daventry's heyday was the 1820's, when the town was a coaching stop and the leather and whip-making industries were at their height. It still retains its market, first granted in 1255, and remains a small but bustling town with its own distinctive character.

The attractions of the Heights are complemented by its rich historical associations. Charles I's defeat at Naseby in 1645 heralded the victory of Cromwell's Parliamentarians in the Civil War, and the king's imprisonment at Holdenby House. Forty years earlier the conspirators in the Gunpowder Plot planned their doomed attempt to blow-up the Houses of Parliament at Ashby St Ledgers, the home of the Catesby family. Elsewhere a string of notable stately homes stretch across the countryside, of which the most well-known is perhaps Althorp House – the home of the Spencer family and where the Princess of Wales spent her childhood.

The half-timbered Elizabethan gatehouse, Ashby St Ledgers, still romantically associated with the Gunpowder Plot. Robert Catesby (1573-1605), still embittered by the treatment he and his family had suffered under Elizabeth I, and anxious about their possible treatment as Catholics by James I, joined others in a plot to blow up the Houses of Parliament. Secret meetings were held in the room above the gatehouse. To raise funds, Catesby contacted Francis Tresham of Rushton, who pledged £2000 to the conspiracy. His involvement led to the plotters downfall. Tresham lost his nerve and wrote a letter betraying the plan, which in turn led to the discovery of Guy Fawkes beside barrels of gunpowder in the cellars beneath the Houses of Parliament on November 5th, 1605. Catesby and his companions immediately fled, first from London to Ashby, then on towards Wales. They were finally caught at Holbeach in Staffordshire, where Catesby and another conspirator were killed by the same bullet whilst standing back to back.

Left The memorial cross in Daventry Market Place to Colonel Edmund Charles Burton (1826-1907), whose most important claim to fame is as the winner of the first ever National Hunt Steeplechase at Market Harborough in 1860.

Right The Moot Hall, Daventry, a superb example of a Northamptonshire ironstone building. Standing in the Market Square and built in 1769, the Moot Hall and nearby neo-classical church dominate this Georgian area of the town.

Lower left The Spencer Estate, Althorp, with St Mary the Virgin, Great Brington, in the distance.

Althorp House in winter. In a county well-known for its 'squires and spires', Althorp House, situated off the Northampton to Rugby road, is probably the most famous. The house is the home of the Earl and Countess Spencer and the childhood home of Her Royal Highness The Princess of Wales. There was a small house here in 1508 when the estate was bought by John Spencer, a sheep farmer from Warwickshire. He created a 300 acre park, built a red-brick house surrounded by a moat and formal garden. Over the centuries the house has been extended and remodelled, the moat filled in and the gardens redesigned. The house now stands impressively in thousands of acres of parkland and is regularly open to the public. Generations of Spencers have been avid collectors of paintings, porcelain, furniture, books and portraits, leaving a collection unparalleled in a stately home.

Left St Mary The Virgin, Great Brington, and the pageantry of the Spencer Chapel. The church was built in about 1200, but after his purchase of Althorp in 1608 John Spencer set about rebuilding the chancel and adding the north chapel to house memorials to himself and his descendants. For sheer spendour and richness there are no other monuments to match them in the county. There are five pairs of full-length effigies lying on canopied altar tombs, as well as a host of other monuments. Perhaps the oddest is that of Sir Edward Spencer squeezed into a funerary urn too small for his feet. An interesting local tradition declares that Charles I made his communion in St Mary's during his imprisonment at Holdenby House in 1647.

Opposite page A narrowboat passing through farming country on the Grand Union Canal near Welford.

Right The gatehouse of the Royal Military Depot at Weedon Bec. The original buildings were begun in 1803 to house a barracks, powder magazine and refuge for the royal family at a time when Napoleon threatened invasion. Weedon Bec was chosen because it lay close to a canal and Watling Street, and was as far away from the sea as possible. The Depot buildings were linked to the Grand Junction Canal by means of a 'cut', protected by a portcullis. The coming of the railways improved access to the Depot, which continued to have an important military role during the First and Second World Wars. The Depot closed in 1965 and several of the buildings were demolished to make way for houses and a factory.

Above Watford staircase lock on the Grand Union Canal near Daventry. The flight of seven locks climbs 53 feet, and alongside are three reservoir pounds used to fill the locks when in operation.

Left Narrowboats moored in their winter quarters at Braunston Marina on the Grand Union Canal north of Daventry.

Cottesbrooke Hall, an exquisite example of Queen Anne architecture built in 1702 by a merchant, Sir John Langham, and now owned by Captain and Mrs J Macdonald-Buchanan. The house is reputed to be the pattern for Jane Austen's Mansfield Park, and its treasures include eighteenth century English and French furniture and porcelain and possibly the finest collection of sporting pictures in Europe.

The lovely gardens and grounds are open on certain days throughout the year, and range from water and wild garden areas to formal herbaceous borders.

Two views taken near the road to Market Harborough between Lamport and Maidwell. Although cereals are now widely harvested, Northamptonshire was once best known for wool. Its flocks grew steadily from the sixteenth century onwards, and by 1800 it was estimated that with 640,000 sheep the county was second only to Lincolnshire as a producer of long wool. It is no coincidence that the same period marked the rise of the 'landed gentry'.

Visible on the hill in the left hand photograph is Lamport Hall, home of the Isham family until 1976 and prosperous sheep farmers during the sixteenth century.

The village of Creaton sits alongside the A50 Northampton to Leicester road on a ridge overlooking the valley below. The village clusters round its Green. Creaton House and Dial House in the High Street are both Georgian, whilst the more recent modern development stretches either side of the country road to Brixworth. The plan of the Saxon village green has survived in several places around the county, but the form of many has been disguised by later encroachment. Originally the central green was where livestock were driven in times of danger, the surrounding cottages and fenced enclosures acting to form a stockade.

The memorial monument on the Pitsford to Brixworth road to Lord Chesham, who died after a fall whilst riding with the Pytchley Hunt in 1907. Sadly defaced, it once read, 'Erected by friends in the Pytchley country. To the memory of Charles Compton W. 3rd Baron Chesham, KCB, who met his death whilst hunting with the Pytchley hounds. November 9th 1907. Aged 56. A good man, gallant soldier, a true sportsman.' There is a second misleading memorial to Lord Chesham near Welton Grange, which although stating to mark the spot where he fell has been moved from the scene of his accident at Monksmoor Farm near Daventry.

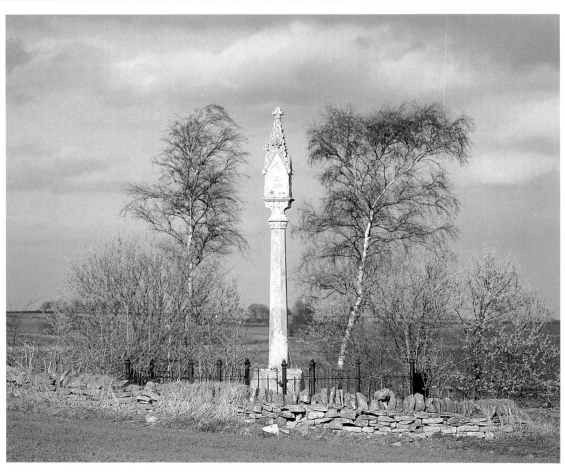

The Elizabethan Arches, Holdenby. The two original gateways of the outer courtyard of Sir Christopher Hatton's mansion of 1583 are all that remain of what was once the largest house in England. Hatton was a favourite of Elizabeth I, who made him Lord Chancellor, and he was known as the 'Dancing Chancellor' because of his love for music and dancing. Hatton also bought Kirby Hall before it was completed and it is thought that Holdenby was sold after his death to James I because the third Sir Christopher could not afford to maintain both houses. Holdenby was demolished in 1651, and in 1887 was replaced by a new much smaller house on the same site, incorporating the old original offices.

The Battle of Naseby Monument, which commemorates perhaps the most decisive battle of the Civil War – the victory of Oliver Cromwell and the Parliamentarians over Charles I and the heavily-outnumbered Royalists on June 14th, 1645.

The battlefield site lies in open countryside to the north of the village of Naseby, and the monument was erected in 1936 after it was found that the obelisk put up in the nineteenth century on the Naseby to Clipston road was standing in the wrong place. There is an unproven legend that Cromwell's dying wish was to be buried on the battlefield, and that after his death his body was brought to Naseby and secretly buried nine feet beneath the site of his victory.

Two views of the dramatic re-enactment marking the 350th Anniversary of the Battle of Naseby by over 3000 members of the Sealed Knot Society in June 1995.

Opposite page Contrasting seasons and times of day at Pitsford Reservoir. Walks, fishing, sailing, picnics, woodlands, nature reserves and bird life enhance its setting in a valley between Pitsford and Brixworth. The waters are the winter home for about a thousand waterfowl, including tufted duck, pochard and shovelars. The 750 acre reservoir was opened in 1956 by Queen Elizabeth the Queen Mother.

Below Walgrave buttercup meadow, well-known in the village for its lovely splash of summer colour.

Harlestone, Upper Harlestone and Lower Harlestone are all attractive villages lying in the shadow of the Spencer Estate at Althorp: shown here are Harlestone and Lower Harlestone. All three lie in the folds of the Northamptonshire Heights amidst woods and pasture looking down on Harlestone Lake. Despite the closeness of Northampton, the area is a beautiful part of the county and deservedly popular with walkers.

A group of thatch and stone cottages in Boughton, on the northern outskirts of Northampton. The village first developed on the edge of a triangular-shaped field known as Boughton Green. Tradition has it that after the Black Death the villagers moved a mile down the road to their present site, leaving behind the old parish church of St John the Baptist – now in ruins, and enveloped in ghost stories – adjacent to the green. For centuries Boughton Green was the home of one of the largest horse fairs in the country, the last of which was held in 1916.

The village of Whilton stands almost at the centre of England, and in some ways this photograph of the surrounding open landscape does evoke the rural heartland. Yet appearances can be deceptive, for within not much more than a mile are Watling Street, the Grand Union Canal, the London to Birmingham railway and the M1 motorway – all of them stressing the importance of the area as a centre of communications right back to the Roman period.

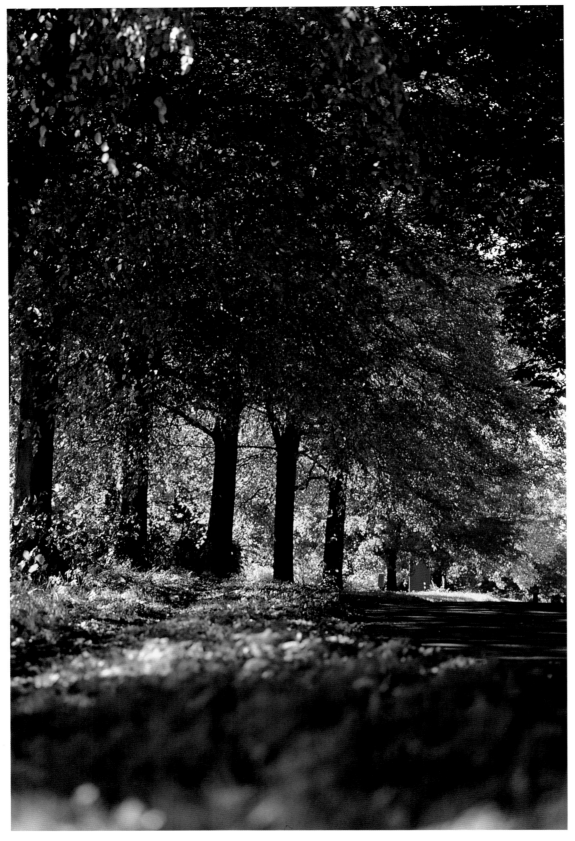

Left Hanging Houghton, north of Brixworth, a small wooded hamlet which literally hangs on a spine of land by the Northampton to Market Harborough road.

Below Lambing at Overstone Grange Farm, Moulton.

Right A line of traction engines braving the damp at Hollowell Steam Rally, held every year in July.

Below right Laying a traditional thorn hedge at Merry Tom Lane, between Chapel Brampton and Spratton.

Below The gate to Holly Lodge, Moulton, complete with a range of farming implements. The castellated style Elizabethan house is the home of the Jeyes family, whose most famous member, Philadelphus, invented the disinfectant still bearing his name.

Moulton Morris Men dancing in the centre of the village at midday on Boxing Day as part of the Christmas festivities. Moulton used to have a traditional Mummers Team performing their plays at Christmas in local inns, a tradition which has recently been revived. Although the group dance throughout the year around the country, the main local festivities incorporate a week of village celebrations during May. On Festival Saturday a May Bower competition precedes the crowning of the May Queen and her attendants, who then go in procession through the village on the May cart, decorated out with May blossom and bowers and pulled by the Morris dancers.

Carey Cottage Museum, Moulton. William Carey (1761-1834), one of Northamptonshire's famous sons, moved to Moulton in 1785 and lived in Carey Cottage. He was a Baptist minister who founded the Baptist Missionary Society and later spent 40 years as a missionary in India. Carey was born in Pury End, near Towcester, where the street he was born in now bears his name and there is also a monument to him. At the age of twenty-two Carey was baptised in Northampton in the River Nene, after which he became a Baptist and started preaching. The Baptist community in Moulton was formed in the mid-seventeenth century when meetings were held in the Minister's cottage. The Baptist Chapel was built at the beginning of the eighteenth century and Carey left a flourishing community which still exists today.

All Saints, Brixworth, which after St Martin's at Canterbury is probably one of the oldest churches in England – and certainly the most outstanding Saxon church in the country. Speculative theories as to the date of the original church will probably never be answered: one has monks from Peterborough building it in about 680; another suggests that it was built around 750 by King Ethelbald of Mercia in honour of his friend Boniface. The latter theory would tie in with the 'relic', thought to be the larynx bone of St Boniface, which sits in an iron cage by the pulpit. Ultimately what matters is the building itself, a model of simplicity and space, which one scholar has called 'the most imposing architectural memorial of the 7th century north of the Alps'. The battlements and spire are of course medieval, but the original Saxon church was even larger than it is today. The stair-turret, added in the ninth or tenth centuries, is one of only a handful left in the country, whilst the circular apse at the east end is famous for its sunken passage running around the outside, which was probably used by pilgrims.

St Andrew's Church, Great Cransley, soars above
the trees on the edge of Rockingham Forest, a few
miles south of Kettering.

ROCKINGHAM FOREST
CORBY AND KETTERING

ROCKINGHAM FOREST
CORBY AND KETTERING

AFTER rising on the Northamptonshire Heights the River Welland flows slowly north into its broad valley. The valley is majestically overlooked by Rockingham Castle, and bridged by the Harringworth Viaduct, whose 82 arches stretch three-quarters-of-a-mile and still remain one of the great engineering achievements of the Victorian age. Rockingham Forest takes its name from the royal Castle, which was deliberately placed to guard the local ironworkings and a crossing point over the river. Most of the Forest has been felled, and today is a patchwork of hamlets, farms and small villages linked by a common use of the attractive reddish and yellow hued local ironstone.

Rockingham Castle owes its construction to William the Conqueror, and was much used by the early Norman kings. King John was a frequent visitor, but the harsh Forest Law that made certain the Forest deer were only hunted by the king and his court has long since been revoked. The Forest was largely oak and ash, underplanted with maple, thorn and hazel which were regularly coppiced. The Forest's survival was always precarious. Elizabeth I enforced a ban on charcoal-burning to try and conserve timber, but a century later Charles II looked towards Rockingham Forest when rebuilding his navy. Without the protection of Parliament it was no longer safe. A short-lived agricultural boom in the 1840s led to many of the woods being grubbed, and arable fields gradually replaced the glades. Wakerley Great Wood and Finshade Woods in the northern corner of the county are wonderful remnants of the ancient forest, with a mixture of coniferous woodland, picnic areas and forest trails.

The ironstone beds in the north of the county have been quarried for building materials for over 2,000 years, but only in the last 200, with the invention of a means of extracting the ore, has their exploitation had any real impact on Northamptonshire's character. This is most evident at Corby, once an obscure village, whose population expanded from 1,400 in the 1920s to 50,000 by the end of the 1960s. But Corby's fall has been as swift as its rise. Faced with a decline in the quality of the local ore, combined with a decline in the iron and steel industries, the furnaces that brought the town its prosperity have gradually been shut down, and its days as a steel town are now over.

The story of Kettering is not unlike that of Corby. Its history is much longer, for it is an old market town with a thirteenth century charter, but its recent past has been dominated by a single industry – the making of boots and shoes. But cheap imports and mass-production have had their impact, and only a small amount of shoe-making still continues in the town.

Previous page The Welland Valley from near Rockingham Castle. The county boundary follows the course of the River Welland along much of the north and west.

A lone oak on the high ground above the Welland Valley serves as a reminder of the last remnants of the ancient Rockingham Forest, which at its largest in the Middle Ages spread as far south as Salcey Forest, covering nearly a third of the county.

Opposite page Rockingham Castle from the air. The site was possibly used by the ancient Britons as a fortress and it was certainly a Saxon stronghold – which William the Conqueror ordered to be converted into a castle soon after the Conquest in 1066 to guard the river valley. For 500 years the Castle was a royal residence used regularly by medieval kings as an administrative centre and hunting lodge to Rockingham Forest, which then covered vast areas of the county. King John was a frequent visitor, in 1216 leaving behind the iron chest now standing in the Great Hall. During the fifteenth century Rockingham Castle declined in importance as the affairs of state became too complex and the monarchy became based in the south. In 1530 a local landowner, Edward Watson, leased the Castle from Henry VIII. Edward started a restoration programme and eventually his grandson, Sir Lewis Watson, bought the freehold from James I in 1619.

Below Rockingham Castle's Norman towers dominate the gatehouse. The Castle fell to the Roundheads during the Civil War, and now only the walls, moats, and some of the stonework remain from the original building. The majority of the house is Elizabethan, whilst the successive generations of Watsons to live in it since 1530 have gradually restored, rebuilt and added to the original plan.

Following page (left) Rockingham village. Thatched cottages, standing in the shadow of the Castle and some two or three centuries old, stretch down the steep hill to the Welland Valley.

Following page (right) Harringworth Viaduct dominates the Welland Valley landscape and although an immense engineering achievement it obscures the attractions of the valley. Built between 1874 and 1879, the 82 arches of the three-quarters-of-a-mile long viaduct originally carried the old London Midland Railway over the valley.

Left A symbolic reminder of Corby's former prosperity, the statue of a steel-worker standing proudly in the centre of town. Corby's ironworks were established in 1910, and by the late 1920's Stewarts and Lloyds were in the forefront of the production of pig iron and steel from iron ore. For well over forty years the night sky around Corby glowed with the reflection of molten iron being cast into pig beds from the iron furnaces, dramatically transforming the local landscape. The little village of Corby became a 'new town' as over 2000 houses were built for the steel-workers, many of them from Scotland. The original decision to locate the steel works in the middle and not the edge of the ironstone bed meant that the new residential areas were in the south-west, away from the factories. By the early 1980's the factories were closing as the industry declined. Government and other initiatives have helped bring employment to the locality, but it is still a depressed area.

Right Corby Market, ringed by new development. The origins of the town are uncertain, but by 1066 the former Viking settlement was a judicial and administrative centre. It remained a small community with perhaps 700 inhabitants earning a living from farming and weaving until well into the nineteenth century. The arrival of the railways in the 1870s encouraged brick-making from the local clay, and the extraction of iron from the ore on which the village stood soon followed.

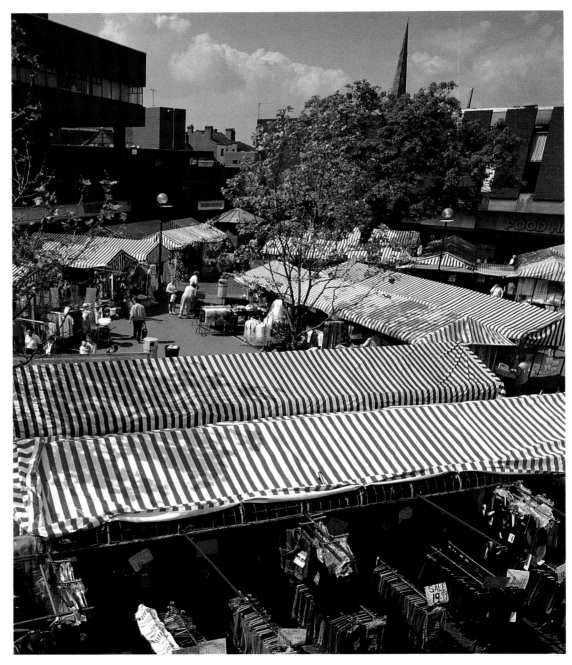

The medieval fourteenth century bridge spanning the River Welland at Duddington. The village is a protected conservation area, and its seventeenth and eighteenth century cottages and houses make it one of Northamptonshire's prettiest villages. The twelfth century church is unusual in that its tower stands on the south side – possibly because the ground at the more traditional west end falls away towards the river.

Looking across the Welland Valley towards
Leicestershire from St Mary Magdalene,
Cottingham. Aptly, the church is built of the local
ironstone, whilst the pillars in the north arcade
have capitals carved with curious human figures.

Left Sheep Street, Kettering, and the scene of the thrice-weekly market since the town was granted its charter in 1227. Of the seventy or so stallholders who now cry their wares, one, a florist, can claim three centuries of continuous family trading! This is the old part of Kettering, showing the houses opposite the market and the Old Market Inn.

Below left Carey Mission House, Lower Street, Kettering, now flats for the elderly but originally the meeting place for the founding of the Baptist Missionary Society by William Carey and Andrew Fuller in 1792. Then living in the house opposite was Thomas Gotch (1748-1806), who as well as financing Carey's studies started the first shoe and leather business in Kettering. Carey also supported himself by cobbling, often walking the sixteen mile round journey from Moulton to Kettering and back again with a bundle of finished boots as a way of earning a few extra pence.

Below Also in Sheep Street, Kettering, are the old almshouses, originally a hospital, built in 1688 with a legacy by Edmund Sawyer.

Wicksteed Park on the outskirts of Kettering is known throughout the world for its park and family amusements. Covering 147 acres and circled by its own railway, it is large enough to escape the screams of fear and delight of the children enjoying its pleasures. The park opened in 1921 as the creation of Charles Wicksteed, who wanted to provide the people of Kettering with 'a place of recreation, an object in their walks, and a safe and happy playground for their children'. In front of the pavilion is the statue of Jerry, a small terrier who was Charles's constant companion.

The Charnel House, Holy Trinity Church, Rothwell. In about 1700 a workman raised a floor slab in the south aisle of the church and discovered the vaulted roof of a thirteenth century crypt. Further investigation revealed a two-bayed room with a fresco depicting the Resurrection and the heaped skulls and bones of about 1500 people. Uncertainty surrounds this extraordinary if grisly collection. Are they the remains of Danish invaders, victims of the Black Death, corpses taken from open graves, or casualties from the Battle of Naseby? The only other similar charnel house is at Hythe, in Kent, and both pose more questions than they answer.

The Triangular Lodge is perhaps the most famous and only completed folly built by Thomas Tresham (1545-1605) – the Elizabethan eccentric. Situated north-east of Rothwell in the village of Rushton, it is almost as curious as its creator. For Tresham was a Catholic in a Protestant age who chose to express his faith by leaving an architectural legacy intended to secretly state his beliefs. A member of the establishment knighted by Elizabeth I, he still managed to spend 15 years in prison or under house arrest. The Triangular Lodge is immensely complex and obscure, but at its simplest is a symbol of the Holy Trinity based on an equilateral triangle. It has three sides and storeys, and three windows on each side of each floor. Three gables on all the sides rise to three pinnacles and a frieze 33 feet long with 33 letters on each frieze. The walls are covered with symbolic dates and inscriptions. Tresham designed the Lodge in his prison cell and built it following his release in 1593 in the grounds of his home, Rushton Hall.

Left The first of Thomas Tresham's buildings to be started (though the last to be finished) was the Market House at Rothwell, where he was lord of the manor. Its theme is friendship, hence the coats of arms of 90 Northamptonshire families running round the frieze beneath the parapet. The Market House remained unfinished at Tresham's death in 1605 and was only finally roofed in the nineteenth century.

Below Lyveden New Bield, another of Tresham's eccentric designs, was built in the shape of a Greek icon decorated with religious symbols to symbolize the five wounds of Christ. It has five equal squares and at the end of each projecting square is a large bay with five faces.

The huge Elizabethan dovecote standing isolated in open fields at Newton-in-the-Willows. Reputed to be the largest surviving dovecote in Britain, it was built out of limestone with a roof of Collyweston slates in the sixteenth century by another more traditional member of the Tresham family, Maurice. It is in excellent condition with over 2000 nesting holes, but the house where this branch of the Tresham family lived has long since disappeared.

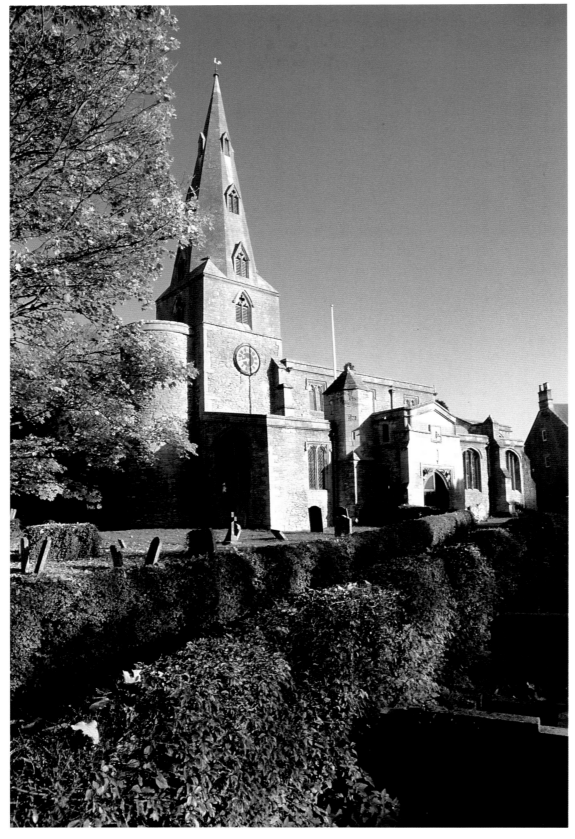

The Saxon church of St Andrew's, Brigstock, which dates back to about 850 and includes the magnificent and rare stair-turret, clearly visible to the west of the tower. The glorious screen in the north chapel is said to have come from Pipewell Abbey when it was pulled down after the Dissolution in 1548. Over the porch there were once living quarters for the monks from Cirencester who administered the church for much of the Middle Ages.

The shadows of Brigstock's medieval market cross cast on one of the stone houses in the centre of the village. Brigstock grew from a Saxon settlement in a forest clearing to one of the largest villages in the Royal Forest of Rockingham. King John stayed in the manor with his court in 1207, which was then a hunting lodge.

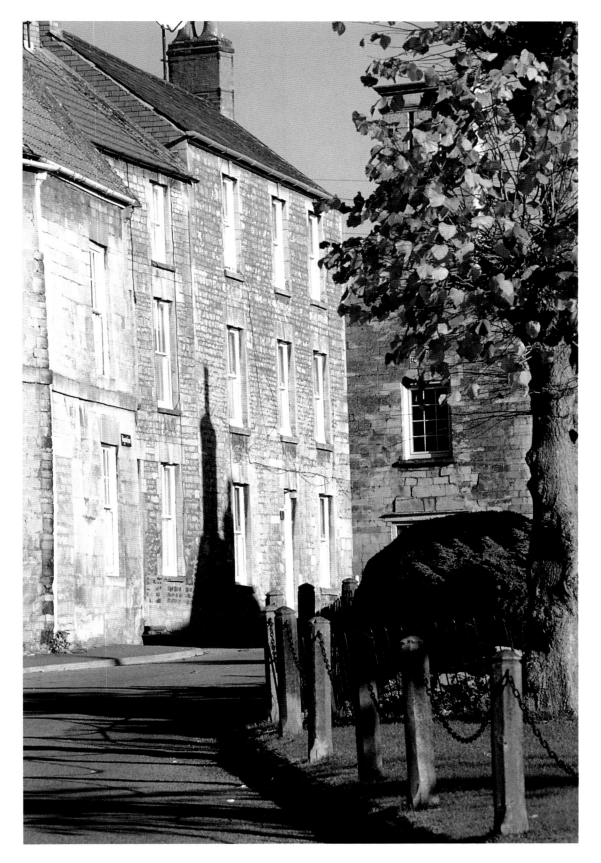

Right Queen Eleanor Cross, Geddington, the second of the two crosses in Northamptonshire built by Edward I as a memorial to his queen. For more detail on the Eleanor Crosses see the text to the Hardingstone Cross on page 20.

Below The Old Hospital, Weekly, showing the painted sundial. Originally built in 1611 by the Montague family in accordance with a law passed during the reign of Elizabeth I to provide, 'hospitals, bidings or working houses for the poor', it originally housed seven poor men with two women to look after them. The coat of arms below the sundial are those of the Montagues, from whom their Weekly estates passed by marriage to the Duke of Buccleuch at the end of the eighteenth century.

Above Thatched cottages in the village of
Sudborough, which lies close to the heart of old
Rockingham Forest and huddles near the main
Thrapston to Corby road.

Right The old circular toll house, Sudborough,
was once part of an extensive network of
eighteenth century turnpikes covering much of the
county.

Right Part of the stained glass window in St James' Church, Grafton Underwood, dedicated to the memory of 1579 members of the American Eighth Air Force who gave their lives while serving at the local airbase during the Second World War. The window was dedicated in 1983 as a gift from veterans, families and friends of the 384th Bombardment Group. Dominating the design is the Boeing B-17 Flying Fortress which the group operated from the base. The crossed flags signify the combined efforts to defeat a common enemy.

Below Rose Cottages, Pipewell, between Kettering and Corby. The village, situated in the middle of Rockingham Forest, is perhaps best known as the site of a Cistercian monastery founded in 1143 and once one of the wealthiest in the country. It was in Pipewell Abbey that Richard the Lionheart met with his nobles in 1189 to plan the 3rd Crusade. The Abbey was destroyed after the Dissolution in 1534 and the tiny aisleless church is said to have been built with some of the stone.

Kirby Hall was built during the Elizabethan age then gradually allowed to decay, so that by the end of the nineteenth century its contents had been sold, it had been stripped of its roofs, and the once exotic gardens were an overgrown wilderness. Kirby Hall was begun in 1570 by Sir Humphrey Stafford, but following its sale to Sir Christopher Hatton in 1575 it was owned by his descendants or the

Finch-Hattons until 1930. In the inner courtyard are the remains of the original Tudor mansion, which Inigo Jones altered by embellishing the already ornate porch and loggia. Walking through the Great Hall, parlours, Library and Long Gallery one still gets a sense of a grandeur and elegance that recent renovation work has done much to revive.

Above St Mary's Church, Weldon-in-the-Woods, in the heart of what was once Rockingham Forest, has an unusual domed lantern on the top of the tower, which continues to be lit with candles on New Year's Eve. Local folklore tells of a traveller lost in the Forest who made his way to safety by seeing the church, and who afterwards financed the building of the domed lantern as a thank-offering.

Left Looking across the lake formed by damning the Willow Brook at Deene House and park, the home of the Brudenells since 1514. In 1661 Sir Thomas Brudenell was created the 1st Earl of Cardigan and it was the 7th Earl, James, who led and survived the famous Charge of the Light Brigade at Balaclava in 1854 during the Crimean War. The house, which is open to the public on certain days, contains a collection of Crimean memorabilia, including uniforms, medals and the stuffed head of Ronald, the horse the 7th Earl rode during the Charge.

Blatherwycke's bridge with its datestone of 1656 provides the backcloth to an almost idyllic setting in this quiet village. The area was once dominated by the Stafford and O'Brien families. The two families intermarried, and stones depicting their intertwined love knot are still visible on the bridge and the nearby entrance to the now demolished Blatherwycke Hall.

The enigmatic figure of a lone archer standing in a field at Blatherwycke: to find it take the Bulwick road out of the village to a sharp right-hand bend and then follow the bridleway on the left. A variety of stories surround this Greek figure, the most common suggesting it to be the memorial to a pet. Another claims it as the Apollo Belvedere, which once stood alongside two similar statues in Blatherwycke Hall.

Looking over the fields to Easton-on-the-Hill with the fifteenth century tower and tall pinnacles of All Saints Church surrounded by trees.

The Priest's House, Easton-on-the-Hill, built around 1500 of local stone under a roof of Collyweston slates, is a rare example of a pre-Reformation priest's house. Designed initially as the residence for a solitary celibate priest, it is thought to have ended its days as a barn or stable. In 1963 the building was saved from demolition by the then rector and the Peterborough Society, who fought for its purchase and restoration by the National Trust.

The village of Collyweston lies on the western scarp of a limestone ridge which drops steeply to the Welland Valley. The name is synonymous with the grey stone slates produced in the village, and still made by a handful of craftsmen. Its source is an underlying bed of slate, which has been quarried since as early as the fourteenth century: before a visit by Edward III to Rockingham Castle seventy-six shillings were paid for 9500 stone slates from 'Colyn Weston'. Originally the slate was quarried from the bed during winter, so that water freezing in the fissures would expand and allow the stone to split naturally. A chisel-ended 'cliving hammer' was used to tap around the edges and finish the splitting, a 'dressing hammer' helped shape the slates, and a 'bill' completed the task by pecking holes for nails near the head of the slate.

THE NENE VALLEY

THE NENE VALLEY

EOGRAPHICALLY the Nene Valley is one of the dominant features of the county. It owes its appearance to the last Ice Age, when enormous amounts of melting water were suddenly released, chopping the tops off the hills. Rising south of Daventry at Badby, and coming off the Northamptonshire Heights, the Nene meanders its way through the main towns – Northampton, Wellingborough, Thrapston and Oundle – before flowing on to Peterborough and the Wash. Much of its progress is across flood plains, once marshes, which were often flooded for long periods in winter and enriched the surrounding fields with their silt.

The Valley's rich alluvial deposits, built up since the last Ice Age, have long been mined for sand and gravel – most notably round Oundle and Thrapston. In the more recent past many of the old gravel workings have found a new lease of life as recreational areas. Barnwell Country Park was established in 1970, and now includes woodland, meadow, marsh and open river – where the vivid turquoise plumage of the kingfishers that breed in the Park can occasionally be seen. Titchmarsh Nature Reserve is also bounded by the River Nene and is a bird-spotter's delight – with migrating waders, geese, plovers, oystercatchers and herons.

Previous page The tranquil backwaters of the River Nene approaching Oundle.

The Nene's rich arable and pasture land, combined with a river navigable from the North Sea, encouraged the early Saxon and Viking invaders to make their homes in the Valley. The result is a legacy of some of the oldest settlements and churches in the county. The Domesday Book survey of 1086 records the area surrounding the Nene Valley as being the most densely populated in Northamptonshire, mainly due to the fertility of the soil. The market towns of Oundle and Thrapston have long provided a commercial focus to the area, with Oundle's church spire rising like a needle above the broad valley landscape. Oundle's charms are as obvious as its spire, and its Elizabethan public school, old alleys and stone seventeenth and eighteenth century buildings combine to make it an almost perfect example of the small provincial town.

The River Nene was navigable up to Northampton as early as 1761, providing a cheap route into the heart of the county for a whole range of goods. But the arrival of the railway and improvements to roads have ended its days as a commercial artery. Today canal boats, small pleasure craft, fishing and walking provide the main activities in this idyllic part of the county.

Opposite page A moody and overcast winter landscape near Nassington. It is likely that the village was originally close to the river on the flood plain, and thus liable to flooding. There is evidence suggesting that the settlement moved to higher ground, where the first Saxon church was built and the present village now stands.

Right The Prebendal Manor House, Nassington, is the oldest inhabited house in the county. Built in 1230 for the Prebendary of the Nassington stall in Lincoln Cathedral it almost certainly stands on a Saxon site. From excavations surrounding the house it is likely that King Canute once owned a royal manor here, probably a large wooden building with a timbered great hall. Further excavations in 1942 unearthed a Saxon cemetery of about 50 graves near to the River Nene. The village church of St Mary's and All Saints has a Saxon nave, whilst inside is a fragment of an early Saxon cross-shaft.

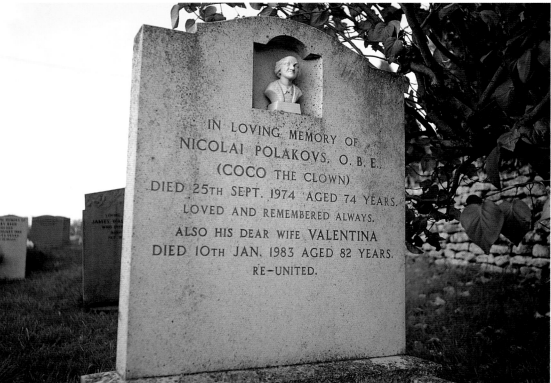

IN LOVING MEMORY OF
NICOLAI POLAKOVS, O.B.E.
(COCO THE CLOWN)
DIED 25TH SEPT. 1974 AGED 74 YEARS.
LOVED AND REMEMBERED ALWAYS.

ALSO HIS DEAR WIFE VALENTINA
DIED 10TH JAN. 1983 AGED 82 YEARS.
RE-UNITED.

Above Looking north across the fields towards Nassington.

Left The grave of Nicolai Polakovs, known universally as Coco the Clown, St Mary's churchyard, Woodnewton. Coco and his wife Valentina retired to the village in 1969 to live near to their daughter. Coco's memory is kept alive by the 'Clownfest' held every other year in the village as a way of raising money for local charities and making sure that the laughter generated by circus clowns such as Coco continues to be heard.

Opposite page The River Nene meandering through fields near Fotheringhay.

The River Nene and the magnificent fifteenth century church of St Mary and All Saints, Fotheringhay. The church was part of a grand plan conceived by Edmund de Langley, son of Edward III, to build a college, which only survived until shortly after the Dissolution of the Monasteries. Either side of the altar are memorials to Edward Duke of York, killed at Agincourt in 1415, and his nephew Richard Plantagenet, who also died in battle, and whose son, Richard III, was born at Fotheringhay Castle.

All that remains of one of England's most historic castles, a rugged piece of masonry from Fotheringhay Castle keep, now surrounded by railings. Embedded in the stone is a plaque to the woman with whom the Castle will always be associated, Mary Queen of Scots – beheaded in it in 1587. The story of Mary is one of the great tragedies of British history. Born a Catholic, and crowned Queen of Scotland aged nine months in 1543, much of her life was surrounded by plotting and intrigue. Finally she was forced to abdicate and throw herself at the mercy of her cousin, Elizabeth I. After spending twenty years under house arrest, she was brought south to Fotheringhay, accused of plotting to overthrow Elizabeth and charged with treason. The outcome of her trial was never in doubt, and in 1586 she was sentenced to death. On the morning of February 8th 1587 she descended the stairs in the Castle's great hall and mounted the scaffold, removing her black gown to reveal a crimson bodice and petticoat, the colour of Christian martyrdom. It took three blows to remove her head. When the executioner raised it by lifting her beautiful auburn hair, it proved to be a wig hiding hair already grey. The final twist came when her dog crept out from beneath its mistress's skirts and lay pathetically beside her corpse. Mary's fate was shared the Castle in which she died. For Fotheringhay was pulled down in 1635 and its stone used by the villagers.

Southwick Hall dates from the fourteenth century when a stone square tower was built by John Knyvett, Lord Chancellor to Edward III. Since then it has been substantially altered and extended by his descendants, the Lynnes, and the Caprons who now own it. The lovely Gothick windows may evoke the early nineteenth century, but it still contains two stair turrets and some rooms from the original house.

Dryden House, Aldwincle, is the birthplace of John Dryden, Poet Laureate between 1670 and 1688. Dryden connections appear throughout the county and in 1551, by marriage, Canons Ashby became the family home. Dryden spent his childhood at Titchmarsh where his mother's family, the Pickerings, owned the manor and his grandfather was rector. Dryden's poetry is now largely unread, and he owed his success to his ability to please whoever he was writing for and manipulate words to suit different occasions. His first published work was a glowing tribute to Oliver Cromwell after his death. A year later when the monarchy was restored, he switched allegiances and welcomed Charles II with equal fervour. He died in London in 1700 and is buried in Westminster Abbey.

Left The country road from Cotterstock to Oundle is dominated by the needle spire of St Peter's Church, Oundle.

Below Oundle's grander buildings and famous public school may help evoke the atmosphere of a small university town, but this photograph of 17th century cottages in Mill Road suggests the network of alleys and yards that contribute so much to its character. Oundle sits on a spur overlooking a giant horse-shoe bend made by the River Nene, and by guarding the river crossing was a regional centre as early as the eighth century. By 1540 six roads converged on the town, bringing trade and prosperity. There is a reference to a monastery founded by St Wilfrid, Abbot of Ripon and Bishop of York, who died in Oundle in 709, but Peterborough Abbey controlled the fortunes of the town from before the Norman Conquest until its dissolution in 1548. Oundle is rich in seventeenth and eighteenth century buildings, all sitting happily together, which combine to give it a reputation as one of the most attractive small country towns in England.

Above Pupils gathered in the courtyard of Oundle School which was founded by William Laxton in 1556. Laxton was a grocer who became London's Lord Mayor, and the school's governors still include the Worshipful Company of Grocers. The school's buildings and boarding houses are scattered throughout the town, and today it is one of Britain's leading co-educational public schools, with about 800 boarders and day-pupils.

Above right West Street, Oundle.

Right The Talbot Hotel in the centre of Oundle is supposed to have been built in 1626 by William Whitwell, but the inn contains earlier features said to have been brought from Fotheringhay Castle – the most notable being the old oak stairway down which Mary Queen of Scots walked just prior to her execution.

A dusting of snow at Barnwell Castle and Manor, the family home of their Royal Highnesses the Duke and Duchess of Gloucester. The Castle was built towards the end of the thirteenth century by Berengar Le Moyne. Its remains, which now largely consist of the massive gatehouse, walls and towers, are open to the public several times a year. The heart of the Manor was built by the second Edward Montagu in 1568, but two additional wings have been added during the last century.

Willy Watt Mill on the River Nene by Kinewell Lake and just outside Ringstead. The mill still has two wheels and was once used for making paper.

Barnwell Mill, now a restaurant, which sits on the edge of its mill pond near the banks of the River Nene in glorious surroundings. There has been a mill on the site since the Norman Conquest, and the present seventeenth century mill only stopped grinding corn after the Second Word War.

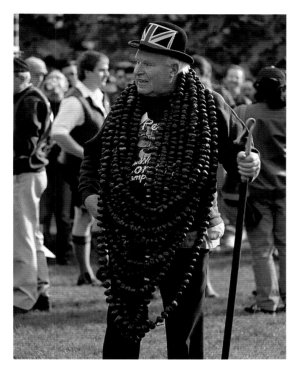

Above King Conker. The village of Ashton has played host to the 'World Cup for Conkers' for the past thirty years. A joyous celebration of English eccentricity, 250 competitors and large crowds – many in fancy dress or from other countries – invade the quiet village of Ashton for a weekend every October.

Right Looking back from Willy Watt Mill at the River Nene. Nearby is Kinewell Lake, once gravel workings, and now a haven for migrating wildfowl with splendid views and a selection of pleasant walks.

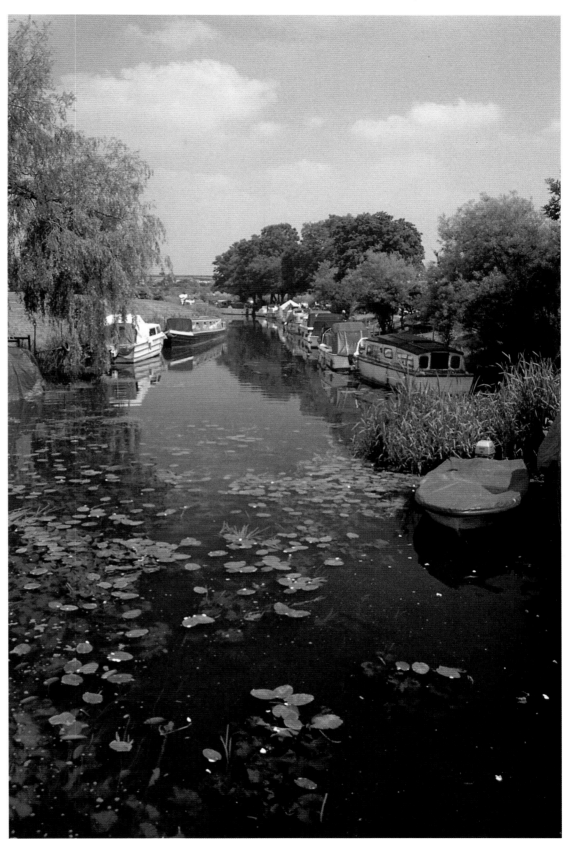

Right Looking across Titchmarsh Nature Reserve and lakes to Aldwincle church.

Below Titchmarsh Nature Reserve, a paradise for all who love the open countryside and the smell of new mown hay. The nature reserve is known for its birds, butterflies, dragonflies and a heronry. Once old sand and gravel workings, the Reserve provides a rich range of habitats – including grassland, deciduous woodland, open pasture and wetland.

Above St Mary and All Saints, Pilton, a typical Northamptonshire view combining manor and spire. In the church are some wonderful late-Victorian tiles decorated with birds, fishes and animals probably given to it by Lord Lilford, the famous ornithologist who lived nearby in Lilford Hall.

Left The Bede House, Pilton, alternatively known as the Watch Tower, and built in about 1515. At first glance it seems unremarkable, but note the curious second floor windows flanked by vertical shafts rising from miniature stone-carved heads. The watch tower projects up from the north gable. According to records the building was originally used as a grain store and a curate's living quarters.

Opposite page top The River Nene flowing beneath trees in the village of Denford.

Opposite page bottom Some of the nine arches of the medieval bridge over the River Nene linking Thrapston with Islip. Records of 1663 refer to it as then having 24 arches, but it was almost completely rebuilt at the end of the 18th century. There was once a crossing toll, from which only soldiers or church-goers were excused. American visitors to Thrapston are common, for Montague House was once the home of Sir John Washington, an ancestor of the first President of the United States. Inside the west entrance to St James' Church is a stone tablet bearing his coat of arms and showing the three stars and stripes from which the American flag evolved.

Two views of the former Corn Exchange, Thrapston. The smaller photograph shows the wooden plough and carved limestone sheaf of corn over its entrance.

WELLINGBOROUGH & THE SURROUNDING VILLAGES

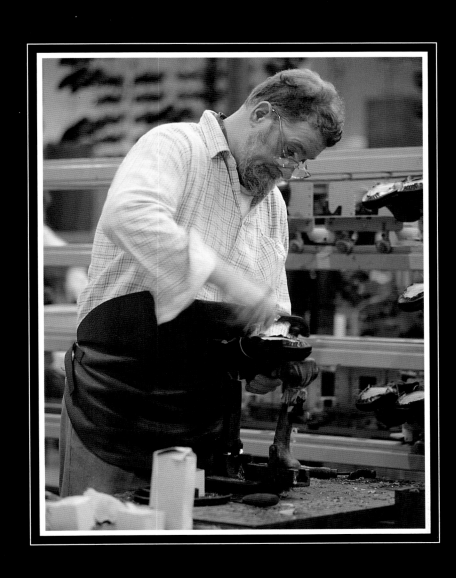

WELLINGBOROUGH AND THE SURROUNDING VILLAGES

WELLINGBOROUGH stands at the junction of the rivers Nene and Ise, and the surrounding district offers a wide variety of attractive country parks, small country houses and manors. Meandering streams feed the Nene, and the villages that follow its course tend to have grown up on ridges or hilltops above the flood plain. The invading Saxons moved up the Nene Valley during the tenth century, and on one such ridge is Earls Barton, famous for Barkers Shoes and for a church blessed with what is generally regarded as the finest Saxon tower in England, dating to about 970 AD. Close by is the even smaller village of Ecton, a place of pilgrimage for Americans, as it is where the ancestors of the great American statesman Benjamin Franklin were once blacksmiths, shoeing horses in a forge behind the Three Horseshoes inn. Once again Ecton's first settlers were Saxon, and it is one of many villages along the Nene chosen because the site combined a defensive hilltop with fertile valleys soils.

Boot and shoe-making in Northamptonshire had their beginnings in the ancient tanning industry, which in turn was dependent on a supply of hides from cattle fattened

Previous page Shoemaking at Barkers shoe factory, Earls Barton. The upper is tacked on by the cobbler spitting tacks into his pliers, lowering the pliers to the shoe and then knocking in the tacks: an amazing feat of craftsmanship, and all done in a single movement!

The Tithe Barn, Wellingborough, situated behind the Hind Hotel and originally used to store the manorial tithes of corn and wool on behalf of Croyland Abbey – whose abbot was Wellingborough's lord of the manor. The superbly restored barn was originally built in the fifteenth century, replacing an even earlier structure.

on the rich grazing lands in the Nene Valley. Northampton was its epicentre, but as the industry gathered momentum during the second half of the nineteenth century it gradually expanded to include Wellingborough, Earls Barton, Wollaston, Rushden, Higham Ferrers, Irthlingborough, Raunds and Finedon. Following the opening of the railway line between Leicester and Hitchin in 1857 the industry eased its way north to include Kettering, Rothwell and Desborough. A further significant event during the 1870's was the huge order placed by the French Government for army boots during the Franco Prussian War. Although the footwear industry continued into the twentieth century, due in part to the need to provide army boots in both World Wars, only at Barkers Shoes in Earls Barton are hand-crafted Northamptonshire shoes still made.

Wellingborough – traditionally a market town granted its charter in 1201 – became a shoe-making town during the eighteenth and nineteenth centuries. The decline of the industry has forced it to reinvent itself as a modern town with light industry and several consumer distribution depots. Sadly, the town's unlikely reputation as a spa is a thing of the past. Yet a visitor to seventeenth century Wellingborough would have been greeted by an abundance of wells, springs and fountains. For the town stands on one of the richest beds of ironstone in the country, enriching its waters with minerals. Some centuries after the event, the poet John Askham (1825 – 1894), who spent all his life in Wellingborough, celebrated the two most famous visitors to drink its waters:

A Royal pair once with their Kingly court
Visited Redwell and drank the healing stream

The royal pair were Charles I and his queen, Henrietta Maria, who regularly visited the town between 1628 and 1637 to sip the chalybeate or sparkling waters that gushed from the Redwell spring.

Below Two views of Sheep Street, Wellingborough. The one below is of what is now a Tudor-style restaurant but was once the site of Wellingborough Abbey, a small monastery belonging to the larger Croyland Abbey near Peterborough, built on land given to the monks by Edred, King of Mercia in 948. The other shows the Golden Lion, built in 1540 and still with its minstrels gallery

Left Wellingborough Embankment. A beautiful and peaceful area where the River Nene flows through the edge of the town. The Nene and Ise join at Wellingborough, and the town is almost surrounded by water.

Below Whitworth Mill, built in 1886 of brick and ironstone was in constant use until about 1959. 7,500 tons of grain a year continued to be brought up the canal in narrowboats from London and then along the Nene as late as 1968.

Below The view from Cogenhoe churchyard looking out over the Nene Valley, with Weston Favell and the outskirts of Northampton in the distance. Cogenhoe has always relied on its larger neighbour for employment, adapting its skills to meet changing needs. Farming and rural trades gradually gave way to railway workers and iron ore miners in the early nineteenth century, and they in turn were followed by the making of hand-sewn boots and shoes in small workshops in the village – which today is the base of Yorks, a large local coach company.

Right The Three Horseshoes Inn, Ecton, is another of Northamptonshire's places of pilgrimage for Americans, for on the site once stood the house lived in by the ancestors of Benjamin Franklin. The Franklins were the village blacksmiths, one of whom emigrated to Boston in 1682, and Benjamin's uncle and aunt, Thomas and Eleanor, lie buried near the north porch of Ecton church. Franklin himself defies easy pigeonholing. Co-author of the American Declaration of Independence, scientist, philosopher, printer, creator of both America's first fire brigade and public library, he remains to this day one of the towering figures of its early history.

The River Nene at Hardwater Crossing looking towards Great Doddington. This is a popular fishing area and nearby is Hardwater Mill, where Thomas á Becket is supposed to have been sheltered by the miller after fleeing from Northampton Castle during his trial in 1164.

Barkers Shoes, Earls Barton. Between 1857 and 1890 almost all shoe-making became mechanised, and Barkers remain one of the few companies still making shoes by hand. Here a leather upper is being stretched over the 'last', enabling it to be attached to the sole. Arthur Barker began shoe-making in a small workshop at the bottom of a garden in North Road, founding the company that still bears his name in 1880. It soon moved to Station Road, and in 1987 Her Majesty Queen Elizabeth The Queen Mother opened the existing 3 million pound factory. Traditional methods are still retained. The shoe uppers are stretched, hammered onto the shoe, and left on the 'last' for five days to dry naturally and retain their shape.

All Saints Church, Earls Barton, stands on a mound in the centre of the village and probably has the finest Saxon tower in Britain, attracting thousands of visitors a year. It was built in 970, possibly on the site of an earlier wooden church. The tower has no buttresses or stairway but pilaster strips – a feature of Anglo-Saxon architecture. These narrow bands of stone project from the surface of the tower, giving the impression of half-timbered framework. In the twelfth century the Earl of Northampton, Simon de Senlis, added the Norman nave, whilst inside there is superb Norman arcading either side of the chancel. The mound north of the church marks the site of a Norman castle.

Left Looking across the fields to Castle Ashby from the road to Whiston, with a flag flying above the turrets of Castle Ashby House, the home of the Earl of Northampton.

Below left Castle Ashby House in the snow. The estate stands in glorious surroundings and has a splendid avenue of trees, planted in 1695 and leading through from Yardley Chase. Castle Ashby has it origins in the eleventh century castle ruins bought by Sir William Compton in 1512. The present building was started in 1574 by the 1st Lord Compton and designed in the shape of an E, whose two arms were later linked by a seventeenth century screen. The stone parapet running around the top of the house spells out in Latin the words, 'Except the Lord keep the house the watchman waketh but in vain: Except the Lord build the house they labour but in vain that build it: 1624'. In 1618 Lord Compton was created Earl of Northampton, and the house remains the family home to this day. Its many treasures include a remarkable set of balustrades on the stairs bearing carvings of animals, trees, flowers and hunting scenes. Although the house is rarely open, the gardens and park can be enjoyed.

Opposite page Hoar frost and a pale sun light up St Peter and St Paul, Easton Maudit. The church contains a monument to Sir Christopher Yelverton and his family. Speaker of the House of Commons in 1597 and a Member of Parliament during the reign of Elizabeth I. Sir Christopher was also a poet whose prayer asking God's help 'to direct and guide us in all our consultations' is still said at the start of each day's parliamentary business in both the House of Commons and the House of Lords.

Opposite page Two views of Brafield-on-the-Green, a busy village divided by the road between Northampton and Bedford. The village green and pond lying away from the main road contrast sharply with the chill but picturesque winter view taken from Denton.

Below The hounds of the Pytchley Hunt in full cry during a January meet at Sywell. The Hunt was founded in the late-eighteenth century at Pytchley Hall by the then Earl Spencer. The Hall has not survived, but the Pytchley remains one of the best-known of all English hunts. Northampton-

shire's hunting squires are the stuff of legend, and include the remarkable Sir Charles Knightley of Fawsley Hall, reputed to have cleared a 31 feet spread of water and thorn on his horse 'Benvolio' at the foot of Brixworth Hill.

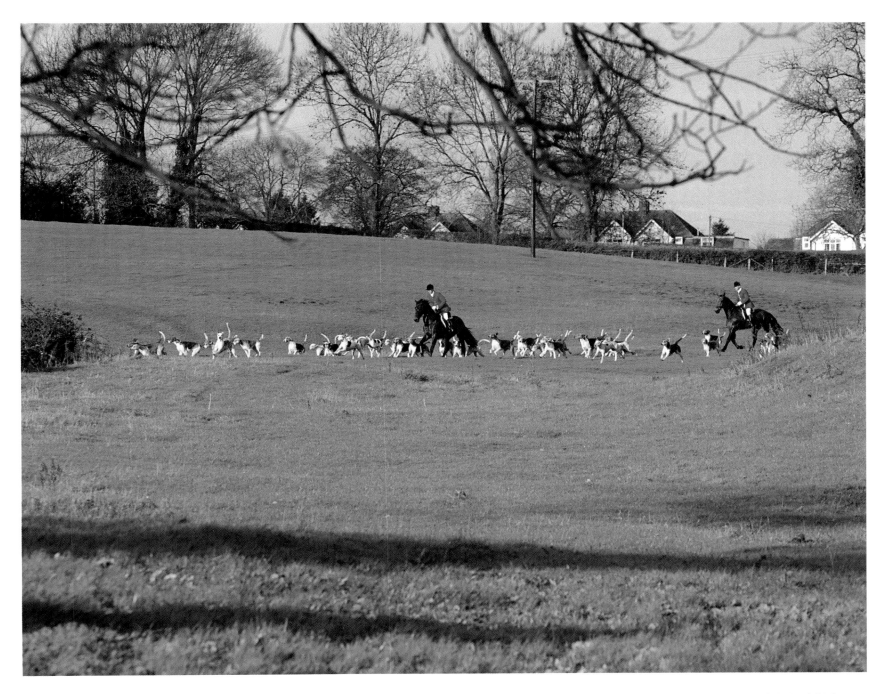

Right Finedon's decorative water tower, constructed between 1903 and 1906 to supply water to the village, and one of a group of folly towers in Finedon built by William Mackworth-Dolben. The others included an ice-house, a series of Gothic arches, Ex-Mill Cottage, and the splendid Volta Tower, which finally collapsed in 1951.

Below The Round House, or Wellington Tower, on the old Finedon to Thrapston road. The house owes its name, and shape, to a visit by the Duke of Wellington to stay with a General Arbuthnot at Woodford House. The Duke apparently remarked on the similarities between the local landscape and that of the field of Waterloo. The general responded by building the tower to celebrate the Duke's visit, incorporating a plaque with the wording:

PANORAMA WATERLOO VICTORY
JUNE 18 AD 1815

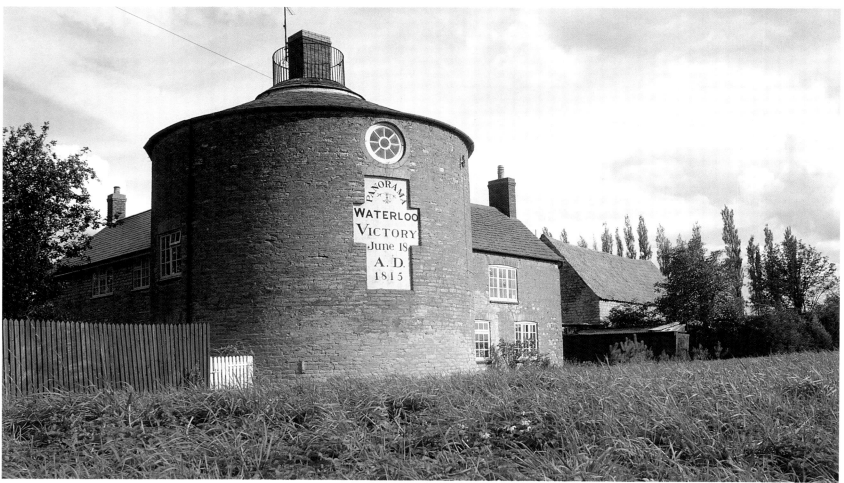

Higham Ferrers may be small, but it hides a heritage typical of many of Northamptonshire's villages. The photograph is of the Chantry Chapel, built in about 1460 as part of a group of ecclesiastical buildings. In the grounds are the medieval church and the Bedehouse founded by Henry Chichele, born in the village and later Archbishop of Canterbury. The Bedehouse dates to 1428 and was home to twelve elderly men whose daily duty was to pray for the king and the charity's founders. Higham Ferrers was certainly Saxon, and later had a Norman castle. Its name stems from William de Ferrers, who in 1251 created a borough with tenement shops grouped round the triangular market place and along the main road – a plan that remains largely unaltered to the present.

A lone angler hoping for a bite at Sywell Country Park, reopened in 1985 on the site of the old Sywell Reservoir. An arboretum rich in rare conifers, picnic meadows and a circular reservoir walk of 2 ½ miles have all been integrated to provide a superb country park used by many local residents. The shallow waters of the reservoir have been allocated as a wildlife refuge, and although limited fishing is permitted and tench, pike, perch and roach are all to be found, any fish caught have to be returned.

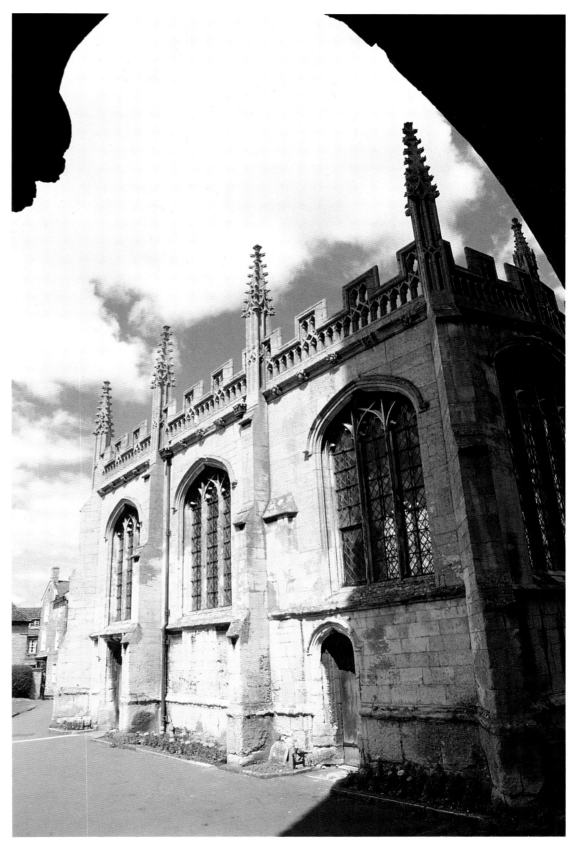

THE PHOTOGRAPHS

Virtually all the photographs in this book were taken specially for it over an eighteen month period in an effort to try to evoke a portrait of Northamptonshire as it is today. All parts of the county have been visited, not only the familiar but also the unknown in an attempt to capture the spirit by which the county is recognised as the 'Rose of The Shires'.

All the photographs were taken using Agfachrome 100 ASA film with the occasional exception when Fujichrome 400 ASA film was used. Two cameras, a Nikon F4 35mm SLR Camera with a variety of lenses ranging from 28mm wide angle, to a 300mm telephoto and a 2¼ Swedish Hasselblad were used. Occasionally a tripod was necessary and a few pictures were 'enhanced' with a polarising filter, or a graduated blue. We hope that the photographs reflect the true nature of the county and its people, and that you derive as much pleasure from looking at them as we did in taking them.

JOHN ROAN, PAUL MARTIN AND PATRICK LEONARD

ACKNOWLEDGEMENTS

Very many people have helped to create this book, and our thanks are due to them all. First and foremost, there are the people of Northamptonshire who are depicted in the book, either wittingly or unwittingly. Then there are those listed below, who have generously provided facilities for photography not normally available. Our principal regret is that we have been able to include only a fraction of the material that has been amassed.

During the research for the book we have talked to many people and we are grateful for their patience and understanding. We must acknowledge the invaluable information gleaned from brochures, guide books and many published works but specific books regularly consulted have included: Ian Addis, *Moments of the Rose*; Chris Billing, *Northamptonshire Curiosities*; Ian Bishop, *Exploring Oundle and Surrounding Villages*; Juliet Smith, *Northamptonshire and the Soke of Peterborough, A Shell Guide*; R. L. Greenall, *A History Of Northamptonshire and The Soke of Peterborough*; Arthur Mee, *Northamptonshire*; Sir Nikolaus Pevsner, *The Buildings of England, Northamptonshire*; John Steane, *The Northamptonshire Landscape*, Peter Gorham Webb, *Portrait of Northamptonshire*.

Amongst those who have helped us we must mention Barkers Shoes; Ian Bishop; Colin Eaton; English Heritage; Express Lift Company; Doctor Hugh Davies; the house keeper – Deene Park; His Royal Highness The Duke of Gloucester and Major Nicholas Barnes; John Harris; Richard Harris; the vicar, Holy Sepulchre Church – Northampton; the vicar, Holy Trinity Church – Rothwell; Captain & Mrs J MacDonald-Buchanan; the Bursar – Oundle School; Northampton Enterprise Agency; Northampton Borough Council – Events Team; Northampton Tourist Information Centre; Northampton Press Relations Team; Henry Sale – Chairman of the Pytchley Hunt Supporters Club; Peter Spong; Mr & Mrs Paisley-Tyler; The Royal Theatre; The Sealed Knot Society; the Earl Spencer; Sutton Sports Photography; Commander Michael Saunders Watson.

Finally our deep and sincere thanks to our families for their tolerance, support and encouragement, without which the book would not exist.

TONY NOBLE, JOHN ROAN, PAUL MARTIN AND PATRICK LEONARD

INDEX

Abington 19
Alderton 39
Aldwincle 101, 108
Althorp 48, 49
Ashby St Ledgers 46, 47
Ashton 107
Aynho 33, 39
Aynhoe Hall 39

Badby 42
Barnwell 105, 106
Blisworth 26
Boughton 63
Brackley 37, 38
Brafield-on-the-Green 122
Braunston 52, 128
Brigstock 84, 85
Brixworth 56, 67

Canons Ashby 41
Castle Ashby 120
Coton Manor 45
Chapel Brampton 65
Charwelton 43
Clipston 58
Cogenhoe 117
Collyweston 94
Corby 76
Cosgrove 28, 29
Cottesbrooke Hall 53
Cotterstock 103
Cottingham 78
Creaton 56
Culworth 42

Daventry 48, 52, 56
Deene House 90
Denford 111
Duddington 77

Earls Barton 113, 118, 119
Eastern Maudit 121
Easton Neston 32
Easton-on-the-Hill 93
Ecton 117
Everdon 43

Fawsley 44
Fawsley Hall 44
Finedon 124
Fotheringhay 99, 100

Geddington 86
Grafton Underwood 88
Grand Union Canal 23, 24, 26, 27,
    51, 52, 63, 128
Great Brington 50
Great Cransley 68
Great Doddington 118

Hackleton 24, 25
Hanging Houghton 64
Hardingstone 20
Harlestone 1, 62
Harringworth Viaduct 75
Higham Ferrers 125
Holdenby 57
Hollowell 65
Horton 27

Islip 111

Kettering 79, 80
Kirby Hall 89
Kings Sutton 40

Lamport 2, 55
Lower Harlestone 62
Lyveden New Bield 82

Maidwell 55
Moulton 64, 65, 66

Naseby 58, 59
Nassington 96, 97, 98
Newton-in-the-Willows 83
Northampton 9, 10, 11, 12, 13, 14,
    15, 16, 17, 18, 19, 20, 21, 22

Oundle 95, 102, 103, 104

Piddington 24
Pilton 110
Pipewell 88
Pitsford 56, 60
Pytchley Hunt 56, 123

River Cherwell 40, 43
River Ise 116
River Nene 18, 95, 97, 99, 100, 106,
    107, 111, 116, 118
River Ouse 28, 29
River Welland 69, 77
Rockingham 74

Rockingham Castle 69, 72, 73
Rockingham Forest 68, 71, 85, 87, 88
Rothwell 80
Rushton 81, 82

Salcey Forest 25
Silverstone 35
Southwick Hall 101
Spratton 65
Stoke Bruerne 24, 26, 27
Stoke Goldington 24
Sudborough 87
Sulgrave Manor 41
Syresham 36
Sywell 123
Sywell Country Park 125

Thrapston 111, 112, 124
Titchmarsh 4, 108, 109
Towcester 30, 31, 32

Upper Harlestone 62

Walgrave 61
Watford Lock 52
Weedon Bec 50
Weekly 86
Weldon-in-the-Woods 91
Welford 51
Wellingborough 114, 115, 116
Whilton 63
Wicksteed Park 80
Willy Watt Mill 106
Woodnewton 98

The Grand Union Canal at Braunston.

The
TEST VALLEY
TAPESTRY

The
TEST VALLEY
TAPESTRY

A unique work of art
depicting the history and
natural beauty of towns,
villages and parishes in the
Borough of Test Valley

Foreword by
Lord Denning

*Introduction and
tapestry descriptions by*
Cyril Pigott

First published 1995 by **Test Valley Borough Council**

© Test Valley Borough Council 1995

ISBN 0 952 6946 0 3

Maps reproduced from or based upon the Ordnance Survey Wessex Touring Map
and Guide with the permission of the Controller of Her Majesty's Stationery
Office. Crown copyright © All rights reserved.

Designed and typeset by BAS Printers in Adobe Janson and Monotype Gill Sans.

Printed by BAS Printers Ltd, Over Wallop, Stockbridge, Hampshire

ISBN 0 952 6946 1 1

CONTENTS

FOREWORD *page viii*

PREFACE *page ix*

INTRODUCTION *page 2*

'IN THE BEGINNING' *page 6*

THE TAPESTRY PANELS
Vernham Dean, Linkenholt, Upton,
Faccombe, Hurstbourne Tarrant *page 14*

Tangley, Hatherden, Wildhern, The Appleshaws, Penton *page 20*

Smannell, Knights Enham, Enham Alamein, Charlton *page 26*

Andover *page 34*

Thruxton, Fyfield, Kimpton *page 42*

Weyhill, Shipton Bellinger, Tidworth *page 50*

Monxton, Amport, Grateley *page 58*

Abbotts Ann, Little Ann *page 66*

Upper Clatford, Goodworth Clatford
Barton Stacey, Bullington *page 70*

Chilbolton, Wherwell, Longparish *page 78*

The Wallops *page 88*

Borough Map with Stockbridge, Longstock, Leckford *page 94*

Houghton, Bossington, Broughton *page 100*

Kings Somborne, Little Somborne, Up Somborne, Ashley *page 106*

Mottisfont, Nursling and Rownhams, East Tytherley *page 112*

Michelmersh, Braishfield, Lockerley *page 118*

Awbridge, Sherfield English, Wellow *page 126*

Romsey, Romsey Extra *page 134*

North Baddesley, Ampfield, Chilworth *page 142*

ACKNOWLEDGEMENTS *page 149*

HAMLETS, VILLAGES, PARISHES AND TOWNS IN THE TAPESTRY

Abbotts Ann	*page 68*	Goodworth Clatford	*page 74*	Penton Mewsey	*page 25*
Ampfield	*page 145*	Grateley	*page 64*	Quarley	*page 64*
Amport	*page 62*	Hatherden	*page 22*	Ragged Appleshaw	*page 23*
Andover	*page 36*	Houghton	*page 102*	Redenham	*page 46*
Anna Valley	*page 73*	Hurstbourne Tarrant	*page 16*	Romsey	*page 136*
Appleshaw	*page 23*	Kimpton	*page 48*	Romsey Extra	*page 136*
Ashley	*page 108*	Kings Somborne	*page 108*	Rownhams	*page 115*
Awbridge	*page 128*	Knights Enham	*page 30*	Sherfield English	*page 130*
Barton Stacey	*page 75*	Leckford	*page 96*	Shipton Bellinger	*page 55*
Bossington	*page 102*	Linkenholt	*page 16*	Smannell	*page 28*
Braishfield	*page 122*	Little Ann	*page 68*	South Tidworth	*page 56*
Broughton	*page 104*	Little London	*page 28*	Stockbridge	*page 96*
Bullington	*page 75*	Little Somborne	*page 108*	Tangley	*page 22*
Charlton	*page 32*	Littleton	*page 47*	Thruxton	*page 44*
Chilbolton	*page 80*	Lockerley	*page 124*	Tidworth	*page 56*
Chilworth	*page 147*	Longparish	*page 85*	Timsbury	*page 120*
Dunbridge	*page 114*	Longstock	*page 96*	Upper Clatford	*page 72*
East Tytherley	*page 117*	Michelmersh	*page 120*	Upton	*page 16*
East Wellow	*page 131*	Monxton	*page 60*	Up Somborne	*page 108*
Eldon	*page 108*	Mottisfont	*page 114*	Vernham Dean	*page 16*
Enham Alamein	*page 30*	Nether Wallop	*page 90*	Wellow	*page 131*
Faccombe	*page 16*	North Baddesley	*page 144*	Weyhill	*page 52*
Forton	*page 85*	Nursling	*page 115*	Wherwell	*page 82*
Foxcotte	*page 32*	Over Wallop	*page 92*	Wildhern	*page 22*
Fyfield	*page 46*	Penton Grafton	*page 25*	Woodhouse	*page 28*

BOROUGH OF TEST VALLEY

This map shows the Test Valley Borough/Hampshire
County boundary when the Tapestry was being worked.
Later, in 1992, South Tidworth became part of Wiltshire.

The detailed descriptions of each Tapestry panel include
a map of the local area depicted.

FOREWORD

In June 1990 Lord Denning, an illustrious former pupil of the Andover Grammar School, who lives near the River Test at Whitchurch, opened the first public exhibition of the 'Test Valley Tapestry' in the Andover Museum (formerly the Grammar School building).

FROM LORD DENNING

I wish to commend this book which tells the story of villages and towns in our lovely Test Valley. Good folk in each of these contributed to it.

Our villages in the Test Valley go back over 1,000 years to the days of Alfred the Great. The villagers built their cottages near the river so as to have access to water and to be available for their animals. They got their water from wells. They built churches of chalk and flint. They were a fine race.

The Tapestry is a splendid record of the past and I do hope many will see it and appreciate its beauty and the work that has gone towards the making of it.

It was Laurie Porter who conceived the project and did much towards its execution. It is sad that he did not live long enough to launch this book but he will be remembered as the mainspring of it. It is, in a way, a memorial to him.

Denning

PREFACE

The Borough of Test Valley, so beautifully depicted in the 'Test Valley Tapestry', is one of Hampshire's largest local authority areas covering some 245 square miles. Its population of 102,000 is spread almost equally between the two main towns (Andover and Romsey) and the hamlets and villages in the surrounding countryside.

The valley of the River Test, and its tributaries, forms the back bone of what is arguably one of the most attractive areas in England, rich in history and natural beauty. It is a delight to those who live here and those who visit.

Test Valley District Council came into being in April, 1974, with the amalgamation of the Boroughs of Andover and Romsey and the Rural Districts of Andover, Romsey and Stockbridge. Subsequently granted Borough Council status, Test Valley comprises 56 civil parishes almost all of which are represented in the 'Tapestry'.

The justifiable pride in which the Test Valley is held by the local community is amply demonstrated in the 'Tapestry', to which so many throughout the Borough have contributed.

Test Valley Borough owes a considerable debt of gratitude to all of these people. They would, I believe, be amongst the first to acknowledge that the project, which is a fine and unique example of community cooperation, would not have come about in the first place without the imagination and tenacity of former Andover and Test Valley Mayor, Laurie Porter.

I do hope that you will enjoy reading this book. In my view it encapsulates the character of the area, both pictorially and by revealing significant events not only of the last decade during which the 'Tapestry' was being made, but of past centuries, in a way that no other guide or reference book could achieve.

If you do not live locally the book may whet your appetite to come and find out more. Where better to start than by viewing the 'Test Valley Tapestry' here at Beech Hurst, in Andover?

Finally, I wish to record special appreciation to Cyril Pigott for his very thorough research in preparation for this book, and the introduction and detailed descriptions of each panel; to Robina Orchard for the section on the design and execution of the embroidery; to my Assistant Nigel Sacree for his enthusiasm in 'pulling the threads together' and to BAS Printers Ltd. for their active support and care in the production of the book.

Gerry Blythe

Chief Executive
Test Valley Borough Council

© Crown copyright licence no. LA079715

INTRODUCTION

The Test Valley 'Tapestry' was completed in 1994, ten years after the ambitious idea was initiated by the late Mr Laurie Porter.

While the 'Tapestry' is technically embroidery, alliteration and historical precedent prevail.

By any standard it is a remarkable and impressive example of community co-operation as well as a strikingly beautiful work of art, unique in this country. It will give succeeding generations pleasure and an historical perspective of the area and the age.

Laurie Porter was born and bred in Andover, growing to love the beautiful Test Valley. A schoolmaster, he taught at schools in Romsey and Andover and was actively involved in public life, serving twice as Mayor of Andover Borough and once as Mayor of Test Valley Borough.

It was during his year of office as Test Valley Mayor, from 1983 to 1984, that he first dreamed of capturing the Test Valley in wool and canvas. He perceived the finished work on the lines of the Bayeux Tapestry but in separate panels.

In a paper dated 9th February, 1984, he drew his fellow Councillor's attention particularly to the Bayeux Tapestry and suggested that the natural beauty and rich, varied history of the area should be portrayed in a similar manner. The paper invited discussion by Councillors on the 'feasibility of providing a Test Valley Mural Tapestry for the Guildhall Council Chamber, Andover'.

It was suggested that the project could 'be carried out by voluntary effort over a period of perhaps three or four years'. The whole tapestry would comprise ten panels each 42 inches wide and 24 inches high, three depicting the Andover area, three the Romsey Area and the remainder 'devoted to groups of wards'.

A centre strip of 18 inches 'could display a stylised panoramic representation of the urban and rural Test Valley scene', while a frieze 3 inches wide top and bottom could provide space for historical information not included in the main panel, examples of local industries, flora and fauna and aspects of modern life.

For technical and artistic support, guidance, and encouragement, Mr Porter was very pleased to be able to rely on the capable assistance of local embroiderers Robina Orchard and Meg McConnell.

Laurie Porter

An attempt was made to cost the project, the paper concluding: 'Over a period of perhaps four years the total cost of materials might therefore be between £500 and £600 allowing for contingencies. The "tapestry" when finished, comprising between three and four million stitches, would probably be valued for insurance at several thousand pounds.'

In a prophetic note Mr Porter wrote: 'The project would involve so much voluntary work over so long a period, that it is not worth doing unless the final result were to be the finest possible and of an artistic quality which could not be outdone by any other Borough in the Country.' Councillors were enjoined to enlist volunteers to implement the project.

Realising that he needed to canvass a wider audience he then sent copies of his paper to all the Parish Councils and the Women's Institutes in the area. His persistence fortunately paid off and gradually villages began to respond positively, submitting original sketches to him for vetting. Meanwhile, the Test Valley Borough Council had agreed to finance the cost of materials from its Lottery Fund.

No one could possibly have envisaged that the project would take ten years to come to fruition nor that the final result would be almost twice as large as Laurie Porter's original dream (far too large to be housed in the Andover Guildhall), with nearly every parish in the Borough being involved.

Sadly, he did not live to see the completion as parts of the last two panels were still being worked when he died in May 1993 at the age of 75. The Test Valley Tapestry will be his enduring memorial.

The Houghton, Bossington, Broughton panel being presented to Test Valley Borough Mayor Mrs. Pamela White.

Villages tackled the project in varying ways depending not only on the artistic talents available but also on who should be involved. In King's Somborne it was decided from the outset that anyone should be allowed to help, regardless of experience. The canvas with the design painted on it, went from one village organisation to another, from house to house and to the village school where every one of the 100 pupils contributed a few stitches under careful supervision. In the end about 320 individuals (whose names were recorded behind the panel) had a hand in its production. It was the first to be finished and was handed over in the Autumn of 1987.

At the other end of the scale some were designed and executed by an individual, or a select few. Unable to contemplate the formidable task of producing a whole panel (258,000 stitches!) most parishes worked a third or less, sharing the panel with adjacent villages.

Collectively, they encapsulate an abundance of wildlife and a pageant of history, together with important buildings and monuments, beauty spots, industries, local characters and contemporary events: an incredible visual time capsule.

As the project gathered momentum in the late eighties and more villages were encouraged to participate, Laurie realised that the original time scale for completion was quite unrealistic.

In 1990 he set an optimistic deadline asking for the work to be completed by the end of May of that year. In a ceremony at Cricklade Theatre, Andover, in June 1990, representatives of the tapestry groups handed over their panels to the then Mayor of Test Valley, Councillor Mrs Pamela White.

'This is now part of the history of Test Valley for ever and a day', she said as she warmly thanked Laurie Porter for his 'determination, tenacity and diplomacy in getting the project off the ground and keeping it on course'. Each parish received a full size photographic copy of its panel for permanent display locally.

In the following month the embroidered panels went on public display for the first time at Andover Museum in an exhibition opened by Lord Denning.

Later, they were displayed in Stockbridge Town Hall and Romsey Abbey, enabling 2,000 people to see them and marvel at their diversity and workmanship.

The publicity prompted the very few parishes not involved to start work without delay. Ultimately most parishes in the Borough, including some seventy hamlets and villages, and the towns of Andover and Romsey are represented. Laurie's original dream has been more than fulfilled.

Subsequently, advice having been sought from the Victoria and Albert Museum about framing, the panels were hung in the Conference Suite of the new Test Valley Borough headquarters building at Beech Hurst, Andover. Here, the irreplaceable and priceless tapestries are secure and in a suitably controlled environment and open for public inspection by appointment.

Lord and Lady Denning (right) at Andover Museum, with Laurie Porter and Cllr. Mrs. Pamela White

The Tapestry has spawned a number of projects, including a musical composition entitled the 'Test Valley Tapestry Suite', commissioned by Test Valley Borough Council, with the support of Southern Arts and the Hampshire County Council.

This suite, comprising eleven separate pieces of folk music, was composed by John Kirkpatrick. It was performed on classical and folk instruments in Andover and Romsey in May, 1992, by an ensemble comprising the composer and five other musicians including four members of the Bournemouth Sinfonietta.

Some of the melodies were subsequently adapted for performance by school musical groups. Roger Watson of the Traditional Arts Projects visited each of the seven primary schools associated with the Test Valley School, Stockbridge, working with children to compose suitable lyrics. Sandra Howlett worked with the music teachers in the schools teaching the songs to individual choirs: *Welcome Song* – Broughton; *The River* – Stockbridge; *The Farmer's Life* – Wherwell; *The World Keeps Turning Round* – Wallop; *The Ballad of Lockerley School* – Lockerley; *Grey and Green* – West Tytherley; and *The Tapestry* – Stockbridge.

Test Valley Tapestry Suite Composer John Kirkpatrick (accordion and concertina), Sue Harris (oboe and hammered dulcimer), Suzanne Kingham (violin), Jane Coster (flute), John Ewart (bassoon) and Andrew Baker (double bass)

In July 1993 the Suite, this time performed by a massed choir of children and seven instrumentalists of the Hampshire Music Service under the baton of Richard Howlett, delighted a huge audience at the Test Valley School, which included Mrs Glenys Porter, Laurie's widow.

The music has also been arranged for band performance by local musician Major Ron Berry.

In order to make the Tapestry as accessible as possible, the Borough Council produced full size laminated photographic copies, which have been in popular demand for exhibitions and talks. Full size copies are also displayed at the Council's Duttons Road, Romsey, offices. Awareness of the Tapestry further afield has been stimulated by articles in local and regional newspapers, national magazines and a BBC South Television broadcast. Colour postcards have been produced, which have gone all over the country and abroad.

No-one fortunate enough to be able to examine the Tapestry can fail to be impressed by the astonishing range, beauty and detail of this unique representation of the Test Valley. Everyone connected with it in any way should be intensely proud of their involvement with the project.

'IN THE BEGINNING'

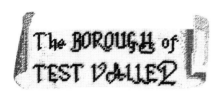

A personal overview of the initiation of the Tapestry, by Robina Orchard

I completed all my embroidery exams shortly before meeting Laurie Porter. He told me about his dream. We both had seen the Domesday exhibition and woodcarving of the Bayeux Tapestry in the Guildhall at Winchester and the idea of portraying the Test Valley in stitches was laid.

I had already used a scene from our village of Amport on one of my exam pieces, but this was not canvas work. The thought of helping with the Test Valley Tapestry was like a magnet. I introduced an embroidery teacher, Meg McConnell, to Laurie. Meg lived locally in the village of Monxton and we had met whilst taking the final part of our exams. Between us we helped Laurie at the launch and throughout the 'surgery' meetings held every few months at the Guildhall in Andover. It was at these meetings that all aspects of the work were discussed including stitches and size of canvas.

Meg and I gave suggestions about tackling design ideas for the main scenes. These were brought to subsequent meetings – ball point sketches on graph paper, beautiful pastel drawings or watercolour paintings by local artists. It was from the Houghton, Bossington and Broughton panel that I chose the colours. We agreed that the centre section should contain a limited selection of stitches whilst the borders should be kept simple using mainly Tent Stitch.

As the centre panels were being worked we decided to have a uniform colour within the borders of all the 'tapestries.' Also the borders should be enhanced by outlining with Long Armed Cross Stitch in blue at the top and green for the lower border with dividing lines in either colour where appropriate. There were no typed instructions so our information was adapted as it was transmitted from scribe to technician!

longarmed cross worked from left to right horizontally

Long Armed Cross Stitch

JOINING

The panels were joined by backstitch into every hole allowing a seam of about four rows. It was suggested that stitching should stop about half an inch from the seam. This allowed for turnings to be folded back and then stitched over to continue the picture. I worked the Monxton, Amport and Grateley panel this way. You will notice that it is quite difficult to detect the joins. Many of the other panels were either worked as a whole canvas or not designed to join as one scene. This problem was overcome by stitching over the join with Long Armed Cross Stitch.

EMBROIDERY STITCHES

These gradually crept in to enhance the scenes. We knew that this would work as the 'tapestries' were to be glazed and hung as pictures. Similar scenes could be used for cushions, stool covers or even communion kneelers, in which case the stitches should be firmly attached to the canvas avoiding loose embroidery stitches.

French Knots were used throughout the panels to depict sheep, flowers, blossom, and in my panel, centre section, as a cow parsley border between

French Knot

the village green and the road. Three colours were used together, yellow, green and white. On the same panel in the Grateley section the horse chestnut flowers were worked quite freely, as were the daffodils scattered throughout the Thruxton, Fyfield and Kimpton panel.

It is always difficult to portray detail in confined spaces and to create with accuracy. Many examples were tried on spare canvas before proceeding. In the Tangley, Hatherden and Wildhern panel the practice paid off as the sewers carefully outlined the tent-stitched cricketers in black stranded embroidery thread giving the players real movement.

Sheaf Filling Stitch was used for the Maypole dancers and for Mrs 'Mac's' fur coat in the Monxton, Amport and Grateley panel. The dresses were white trimmed with blue rick rack. The braids were whipped as was the iron fence of Grateley school.

CANVAS STITCHES

Even to the uninitiated these panels are full of ingenuity and imagination. I hope to highlight some of these interpretations by explaining the variety of stitches.

Tent Stitch

A number of panels have been worked predominantly in Tent Stitch. This gains nothing from light reflections – appearing completely flat like a woven surface. When this stitch is used, colour has been carefully selected to draw our eyes to specific features. This is one of the few stitches which could have given a real feeling of a painting if a little more highlighting had been included. It is a very time-consuming stitch and those sections which were worked by one individual will have taken many hours. The Abbotts Ann panel was worked this way by one person who also selected his own colours – a mammoth task.

Countryside

Fields adorn many panels, and it is their portrayal which particularly intrigues me. I admire the inventiveness shown here: cut and uncut corn, harvesters and tractors, ploughed fields and meadows, cattle and sheep. Perhaps there should have been a pig or two somewhere – there are lots around!

Some stitches represented are Encroaching Gobelin, Brick, Cross, Florentine, Cashmere, Diagonal and Long Armed Cross. The Clatfords and Barton Stacey panel includes an interesting combination of Chain and Brick Stitches.

Florentine Stitch

7

Bushes and Trees

These are worked in many types of stitch. The very effective Cross Stitch, sometimes interspersed with Tent Stitch, gives a little added texture. French Knots are popular, and sometimes are worked quite loosely. For distant trees Hungarian Stitch and an adaptation of Florentine Stitch work particularly well. They both travel quickly over the canvas and with a good blend of colour in the needle instantly depict the subject. However, if it's real detail you like then Leaf Stitch or Fan Stitch are used to their full advantage in a few panels.

Leaf Stitch used for the ear of corn on the Map.

Leaf Stitch

Water

The rivers and streams show very little variety of stitches. Florentine and Brick Stitch variations are the most popular and reflect the glistening ripples of the chalk streams which flow throughout the county. Silk threads have been used with wools to illustrate the jewel-like qualities in the rivers as they babble along.

Sheep

As you pass through this scenic area at certain times of the year sheep dominate the fields. These creatures are portrayed in amusing and devious ways. Some sheep are tidily stitched in Tent Stitch whilst others are shown in their rough dress of tousled wool. Needless to say the varieties of sheep are endless. Some have round faces and tight bubbly curls of wool, whilst others have ringlets and black noses and feet. The 'Test Valley Sheep' as I am sure they will be known seem to have developed their own particular characters.

Detailed tapestry section of sheep

Buildings

Chequered patterns of brick and flint can be seen in many of our villages. Longparish and Kimpton have fine examples. Once again these features have been ingeniously portrayed with blends of thread and imaginative directional stitching to catch the light. Stitches include Smyrna or Double Cross, Flat and Upright and Basic Cross.

Brick houses in this area seem to be generally modern or Victorian. Flint is still used on occasions for decorative purposes. Bricks are depicted using several stitches from Tent and Flat to Straight Gobelin, Hungarian and diagonal – all to excellent effect.

Thatched cottages abound in almost every village. Inventive stitches have been used to portray the rustic properties of the roofs. For the Penton panel Flat stitch was used effectively whilst others developed variations of Encroaching Gobelin Stitch. Stockbridge has used a version of Florentine Stitch for its new golden thatch by the river.

Snow

We do get snow now and again in the valley, although some villages are more exposed than others. Several of us managed to work the seasons into our panels in quite a subtle manner – by portraying spring bluebells with summer flowering roses, autumn blackberries and winter trees. Only one panel (Vernham Dean) shows a beautiful interpretation of snow clad thatches and fields blending into the other seasons. Icicles hang down from the roof in front of the tiny window in the centre of the picture. Rhodes Stitch with an interesting blend of colours is used for the snowy thatch.

Working from photographs and sketches on the Knights Enham, Enham Alamein panel

WORKING FROM PAPER TO CANVAS

Many of the Test Valley canvases were drawn using waterproof ink, sometimes using a photograph underneath the canvas. Outlined drawings on paper can be enlarged on photocopiers.

My experience is that working from a main coloured design and photographs is easier than painting the canvas with oils or acrylic paint. The painted method was used for the Amport section, which was thought to be easier for novices. However, this was not as straightforward as had been hoped.

Inspired by the Test Valley Tapestry, I subsequently worked on another much larger canvas picture. This hanging is bigger than a single bed, being 6ft x 4ft with only an 18in square area of detail worked in Tent Stitch. I used the fast moving Brick Stitch for the remainder. The original cartoon took all my efforts. Laying the canvas over the painting I marked the indicating lines with waterproof ink. The main feature's size was worked out on graph paper. (I mention this should you also feel compelled to put your ideas into stitches, having yourself been inspired by the Tapestry.)

Original colour design for a panel

THE MAP

In order to standardise the size of the Stockbridge panel we agreed that a map of the Borough of Test Valley should be added, so it was almost an afterthought. This had to be worked on 24 threads to the inch canvas. I used Appleton's crewel wool, with pearlé thread for the lettering, and stranded DMC embroidery threads for the coat of arms, compass and lower border lettering.

This was very time consuming, taking about an hour to complete a square inch. I adapted the lettering and experimented with threads of varying thicknesses. I had thought of working it like an old parchment in greys and sepia tones but the coloured one was preferred to blend with the colours of Stockbridge.

The sheep are being driven from Wales through Stockbridge to the Weyhill Fair made famous by Thomas Hardy. I worked from a photograph of the Test Valley Borough coat of arms. The extract from Tennyson's 'The Brook' was quoted by Lord Denning at the first public exhibition at Andover Museum in 1990.

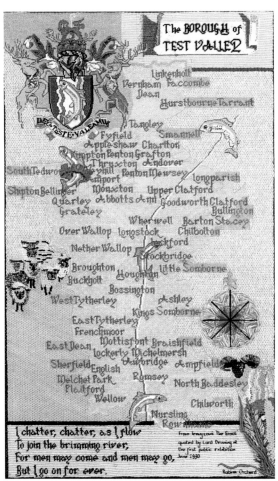

The Test Valley Borough map from the Stockbridge panel

The ram, poppy, ears of corn and compass with its engraved prisms, are all worked in surface stitches. The stitches employed are Byzantine Stitch and a woven Spider's Web for the poppy; Leaf Stitch for the corn; and Chain Stitch with a little Needle Weaving for the grasses.

The ram is in French Knots with Blanket Stitch horns.

You can see that the river rises north-east of Andover and flows out into Southampton Water. It passes through Lord Denning's area of Whitchurch just before entering into the Borough of Test Valley. Many tributaries join it on its journey through Stockbridge with its famous fishing club, indicated by the central trout.

TECHNICAL DETAIL

Appleton's Crewel wools were chosen to enable the stitcher to blend the colours. Short lengths are advised as the canvas wears the threads. Stranded embroidery threads can be used with the wool to give the luminescent effect on subjects like kingfishers, fleshy leaves, fish and rivers. Generally three threads were used in the needle for maximum cover of the canvas. However, this was not a hard rule as some types of stitches required less thread.

SPECIFICATIONS

Canvas	16 threads per inch – worked in frames
Panel Size	Overall 24in x 42in (the width of the finished panels actually varies from 42in to 45in)
Borders	(top and bottom) 3in
Middle Section	18in
Border Frame	Long Armed Cross
Other Stitches	Tent/Half Cross and many canvas stitches including embroidery surface stitches.
Thread	Appletons Crewel wool and stranded embroidery threads.

There were variations on the 'standard' specification, for example, the Test Valley map was worked at 24 threads to the inch: the Abbotts Ann panel has top and bottom borders 4 inches deep, the middle section measures 16 inches; the overall width of the panel is 36 inches and it was worked at 18 threads to the inch.

Typical colour palette for embroidery threads

THE TAPESTRY PANELS

Vernham Dean
Linkenholt
Upton
Faccombe
Hurstbourne Tarrant

VERNHAM DEAN, LINKENHOLT, UPTON, FACCOMBE and HURSTBOURNE TARRANT

© Crown copyright licence no. LA079715

These villages comprise the United Benefice of Hurstbourne Tarrant (St Peter), Faccombe (St Barnabas), Vernham Dean (St Mary the Virgin) and Linkenholt (St Peter). Faccombe is not only the most northerly parish in Test Valley Borough but, at 800 feet above sea level, the highest, commanding wonderful views over the North Wessex Downs into Wiltshire and Berkshire. Its neighbour, Linkenholt, a tiny, remote community little more than a collection of farm buildings, is also rich in scenic beauty. From here the ground falls steeply into Vernham Dean, a parish which embraces several hamlets including Upton. It is here that the Bourne Rivulet has its source although it is the River Swift that flows through Upton to join the Bourne at Hurstbourne Tarrant. Clustered round the pond in the centre of the village are a number of picturesque thatched cottages. Three counties – Hampshire, Wiltshire and Berkshire – meet in this corner of the Test Valley.

Hurstbourne Tarrant was a Saxon settlement (Hissaburnham), part of the extensive King's Forest. In 1266 Hurstbourne was granted to the Cistercian nunnery at Tarrant in Dorset, hence the name. Writer William Cobbett loved the village, staying often with his friend Joseph Blount at Rookery Farm where he wrote much of his 'Rural Rides'. He made more than 20 references to 'the village of Uphusband, the legal name of which is Hurstbourne Tarrant'. In one he commented 'I love this place'. The very large gravestone of his friend Joseph is just inside the lych gate of the church. He left instructions that the stone should be large enough for children to play marbles on.

Top border

Badge of the Women's Institute and the Hampshire Rose; the *emblem of the Game Conservancy*, of which the Faccombe Estate, now some 4,000 acres, is part; *ghost of a cleric* haunting Conholt Hill. Legend has it that during the plague of 1665, the Rector, terrified of catching it, persuaded the victims to assemble on the top of the hill, promising to take them food and medicine. Instead, he abandoned them. But he eventually contracted the disease and succumbed. Many have claimed to see his ghost; the *sign of Manor Farm Dairy*; the *flag of Linkenholt Cricket Club*; the *special stamp to commemorate the engagement of Prince Andrew and Miss Sarah Ferguson*. The *crest of the Mothers' Union*; the *sign of the Boot Inn*, now a private house; the *badge of the Royal British Legion*; *Riding for the Disabled*; *Halleys Comet* which appeared in 1986. The comet is also featured in the Bayeux Tapestry. The *badge of the Girl Guide movement*; the *Olympic Games rings* marking the 1988 games in Seoul.

Middle section

The four churches naturally figure prominently. At the top, towards the left, below the cricket club flag, is *St Peter's, Linkenholt*. This was moved from behind the Manor in 1871. Parts of the old church, including the 12th century south doorway, were retained. The drum-shaped font with tapering sides is Norman. Opposite, on the right is *St Barnabas, Faccombe*. This was built in 1866 of stone and flint in 14th century style. It replaced the smaller church of St Michael in the hamlet of Netherton. The font and some of the memorial tablets were transferred to the new church. The scenery between the two churches represents the view from Vernham Dean church looking up to Linkenholt. *St Mary's, Vernham Dean* is seen below Linkenholt church. The oldest parts are the north wall of the nave and the west doorway, dating from the end of the 12th century. St Mary's was largely restored in 1851 to the design, it is said, of the curate, the Rev J M Rawlings. The fourth church,

St. Peter's Church, Linkenholt

View into Wiltshire from Vernham Dean

on the right, is *St Peter's, Hurstbourne Tarrant* which incorporates a mixture of styles: a beautiful Norman south doorway; 13th century aisles and a 14th century western bay. The tower was heightened with a spire in 1897, made partly of old timbers. On the north wall is a large mural, possibly 14th century representing the 13th century French legend of 'The three living and the three dead', where three kings out hunting met three skeletons which reminded them of their mortality. Another mural depicts the deadly sins.

The open country in the top left corner is the view looking out of Hampshire towards the Iron Age Hill Fort, Fosbury Camp. Just visible is *Dean Cottage* while a *hot air balloon* sails into the sunset. The *batsman* is wearing the colours of Linkenholt Cricket Club whose picturesque ground is situated opposite the church.

To the right of Vernham Dean church is *Vernham Manor House*, a fine Tudor building constructed round an E-shaped timber-framed structure. Extensive exterior alterations were carried out in 1960 and further refurbishment in the 1990s. Between the Manor and the church on its right is *The Square* in Hurstbourne Tarrant.

The *house* on the left was the village shop and post office but is now a private house. The imposing house across the road is *Four Winds Cottage*.

Winters can be very severe in this part of the valley and the wintry scenes are illustrated at the bottom. The *large house* in the corner is the brick and flint 'Always', Back Lane, Vernham Dean. It dates from the 17th century. The present owner says that the village carter lived there and remnants of the stable are in the garden. It was probably also, at one time, an ale-house. On the right is the *George Inn*. A bill of sale of the property in 1847 lists, among other things, 'thatched stable for seven horses, and piggeries adjoining, a flint and thatched granary . . . thatched barn . . . a skittle ground'.

Opposite the George is the *village pump and drinking fountain*, still in working order. This is a good example of the Victorian foundryman's art, water being discharged from the mouth of a lion's head. Seen through the icicles is the thatched *Beeches Farmhouse*. The 18th century timber-framed structure is now masked by rendering. In the

Hurstbourne Tarrant

kitchen is a large brick bread oven. The house was once a doctor's surgery, and operations were performed on the kitchen table.

The building on the right of the icicles was the *Post Office Stores* at Upton. When the panel was designed it was still functioning but is now a private house. The horse in front is *'Bearcone'* from a local stable. Bearcone was especially fond of Polo mints and would always stop hopefully by the shop. In the bottom corner is *Murrle Cottage* with the *River Swift* in full flood in springtime.

Lower border

Ferns (from the old village name Fernham); *snowdrops, hedgehog*; *primroses, badger and fungi, periwinkles, pheasant*; *dog rose, rabbit, blackberries*; *thistle*, with the names of the five villages.

The River Swift at Upton

Tangley
Hatherden
Wildhern
The Appleshaws
Penton

TANGLEY, HATHERDEN, WILDHERN, THE APPLESHAWS and PENTON

© Crown copyright licence no. LA079715

TANGLEY, HATHERDEN, WILDHERN

The parish of Tangley, which includes the hamlets of Hatherden and Wildhern, is situated in the north west corner of Hampshire, most of it in an officially designated 'Area of Outstanding Natural Beauty'. Icknield Way, the Roman road from Winchester to Cirencester, runs through the parish.

Top border

A Roman soldier; coat of arms of the Merceron family which held the title of Lord of the Manor; *an old well* 185 feet deep, reputed to be 350 years old, still used by the water authority to measure the water table; *arms of James Samborne* who endowed Hatherden School; *farm worker* with pitch fork.

Middle section

In the top left-hand corner is the *church of St Thomas of Canterbury*, Tangley, rebuilt in 1872 on the site of an earlier church. The tolling bell is believed to have been cast in 1522 while the early 17th century font is the only lead font in Hampshire. The tower and spire were built by Mr F Merceron in 1898 to commemorate Queen Victoria's diamond jubilee. In the *carriage* on the way to church is Mr Michael Colvin MP, of Tangley House, with his daughter who was married when the panel was being planned. Below the church at the crossroads is the *War Memorial*.

At the bottom left is *Christ Church, Hatherden*, built in 1857. In 1975 it was struck by lightning and completely gutted. A new church was built within the old walls and was rededicated by the Bishop of Winchester in 1977. In the centre of the panel is the *village hall at Wildhern*, built in 1959, and the *playing field*. To the right of the hall is the *Methodist Chapel* built in 1880 from flint and locally made bricks, replacing a nearby earlier building. The white faced building to the left of the hall is *Hatherden Cottage* and, partly hidden on its left, *Oak Cottage*, home of Mrs Griffin who designed the panel. Its TV aerial is the only one in the Test Valley Tapestry. Between the hall and Hatherden Church is *Hatherden C of E School*, founded

Arms of Hatherden School

22

in 1725 by James Samborne for 24 poor children. To the left of the original building is a Victorian extension and, just in view, a modern classroom. Income from a Samborne Foundation still benefits the school and ex-pupils. The *'lollipop lady'*, Sheila Webb, sees children safely across the road. Other houses in the panel are typical of various kinds in the three villages. The *red telephone kiosk* has since been replaced by a modern type while the *low building* behind the *copper beech tree* represents intensive poultry farming. In the bottom left corner is *Maurice Hancocks with Friesian cows*.

Lower border

Woodpeckers caused considerable damage to the shingles on the spire of Tangley Church; there are at least two local *badger* setts; *deer*; a *hen*, representing the poultry industry; *grapes* – there are two local vineyards.

THE APPLESHAWS

The name Appleshaw is derived from Old English 'scarga' – a shaugh or wood; thus Appleshaw may mean 'apple wood'. It includes the hamlet of Ragged Appleshaw, the 'ragged' possibly being a corruption of 'roe gate' – the gate of the Royal Deer Forest of Chute. The northern boundary of the parish is the Wiltshire border.

Top border

The *sheep and the shepherds' crooks* are reminders of the annual Appleshaw Fair which was originally held three times a year: in May for the sale of pigs, and in October and November principally for sheep. In 1801 15,000 sheep were sold at the fair. Local farmers profited by growing turnips for the drovers and dealers.

Middle section

In the top right-hand corner is the church of *St Peter-in-the-Wood* built in 1836. In the centre of the panel is the *Walnut Tree Inn* named for the walnut trees which have long been associated with the village. In 1953 fifteen more were planted to mark the Queen's coronation. To the left of the public

The watch repairer at work in Appleshaw

Church of St Peter-in-the-Wood, Appleshaw

The clock at Appleshaw

Lucinda Green

house is the *village shop and post-office*. Tucked round the corner behind the thatched, bay-windowed cottage on the right is *Forge Cottage*, formerly the blacksmith's shop. A *cricket match* is in progress on the recreation ground, with the *pavilion* in the background. Clutching his bat is the splendidly bearded figure of *Dr W G Grace* who played there at least twice. On July 15th 1870 he played for Danebury against West Hants, taking 11 wickets in the two innings but managing only to score 0 and 14 respectively. One 'six', however, soared over the Ragged Appleshaw Road into Farmer Bailey's field where a thorn tree (now built over) was planted to mark the spot.

On the other side is *Lucinda Green*, formerly Prior-Palmer, the 1982 world champion of three-day eventing, who lives in the village. She is seated on her horse *'Be Fair'*.

In the corner are white *Beersheba daffodils* with their long, narrow trumpets. The bulbs were grown by the Revd G H Engleheart who lived in the village in the late 19th century. Beersheba bulbs, which were reputedly sold to Holland for about £1,000, can still be seen in local gardens.

Lower border

An *apple tree*, symbol of the village; a hoard of *Roman pewter vessels* was unearthed in the parish by the Revd Engleheart in 1897. The find comprised 10 large circular dishes together with numerous other items; they are now in the British Museum; the *local farrier*; a *walnut tree*, one of those planted to commemorate the coronation.

PENTON

Penton ('the farm at a penny rent'), with probably Saxon origins, comprised the twin parishes of Penton Mewsey and Penton Grafton. The Mewsey and Grafton are post-Conquest additions deriving from Maisy and Grestain in Normandy.

Top border

The *arms of the Stonor family* who held the manor from 1346. The *Sanctus Bell* inscribed 'Sic nomen Domini benedictum Ao Xi 1555'. It was discovered in a niche in the wall of the rectory during repairs in 1845, probably having been hidden there during the religious upheavals; a *wooden spade*, typical of those made at Penton for sale at the nearby Weyhill Fair; the *arms of Phillipa Roet* who married Geoffrey Chaucer the poet (1340-1400). Their grand-daughter inherited land locally.

Middle section

In the top left corner is *Holy Trinity Church* probably built in the mid 14th century by the Stonor family to replace an earlier church, mentioned in the Domesday Survey which possibly fell into decay during the Black Death. The surrounding trees are symbolic of many fine local specimens. The knight on the splendidly caparisoned steed represents *Sir Robert de Maisy*, a descendant of the Robert who accompanied Duke William to Hastings in 1066. Sir Robert held the manor from 1233 to 1295 for his liege lord the Earl of Gloucester.

The centre section represents the main section of the village street which ends in a cul-de-sac, giving it a welcome measure of peace and quiet. Outside one of the houses is *a tractor*, symbolic of the village's continuing agricultural heritage. On its left is the sign of the village public house the *White Hart*. The first mention of an 'alehouse' in Penton occurs in the Court Roll of 1431.

In the right-hand corner is a *cast-iron hand pump*, typical of several that survive in gardens in the village. Between it and the inn sign is the prominent *village pond*.

Lower border

On the left is the *small bridge* spanning the stream which usually rises from springs beneath the pond and joins the Pillhill brook at Charlton. On its right are *wild flowers* and *ears of corn*.

Daffodils by Penton Pond

Smannell
Knights Enham
Enham Alamein
Charlton

SMANNELL, KNIGHTS ENHAM, ENHAM ALAMEIN and CHARLTON

© Crown copyright licence no. LA079715

SMANNELL

The name Smannell is thought to mean 'The place of the swineherds', a clearing in the forest where pigs were encouraged to grub out trees and undergrowth. There has been a settlement at Smannell and nearby Woodhouse since earliest times. The Saxons lived here and the Romans before them built two of their main highways through this district, the Portway and Harroway. Now, five roads meet in the centre of the village by the British Oak Inn.

Top border

Skittles, representing the annual village fete and bowling for the pig competition held before the war at Finkley House and then at Postgrove House. Since 1976 skittles competitions at Woodhouse Farm have raised money for charity; the *fifty-pence coin* commemorates Mr Christopher Ironside of Church Farm House who designed Britain's first decimal coinage introduced in February 1971; the *steam engine 'Lincoln Imp'*. This was owned by the People family who ran their threshing tackle business from Jubilee House. The 'Imp', fully restored, is exhibited at steam rallies by its owner, Derek Marder; the *cottage loaf and peel* denote bread making

begun at Woodhouse Bakery nearly two centuries ago and still in production. Until a coke-fired oven was installed in 1920 brushwood served as fuel; *Riding for the Disabled*: The Andover group started at Woodhouse Farm in 1972 with children from Icknield School; the *hurdle* represents three local businesses which supplied hurdles, peasticks, bean rods, faggots and logs. Birch twigs were sent to Crosse and Blackwell for colouring vinegar and bark from felled trees went to tanneries. There is still a fencing business at Little London.

Middle section

The *cottages* in the top left corner are from the hamlet of Little London which was established in 1665 by refugees from the great plague. The *cultivated fields* belong to Woodhouse Farm whose *farmhouse* (on the right) dates from 1746. *Thatched wooden barns* resting on staddle stones were destroyed when incendiary bombs were dropped on the village by a German bomber during the Battle of Britain in September 1940. The thatched building on the left is the *Woodhouse Bakery* which was originally three cottages (about 1640), housing workers engaged in charcoal burning in the surrounding woods. The *red bakers' van*

Smannell

can be detected at the end of the cottage. The *cows* are part of the local herd of Friesians. The *staddlestones* with flowers at their base are from Finkley Manor Farmhouse (1787) which lies astride the Roman Portway. Finkley (from the old English for 'clearing of finches'), was recorded in medieval documents as a woodman's hut in the King's Andover Forest.

The red-tiled building is the *school*, built in 1873 for £324.15.6 and opened with 84 pupils whose ages ranged from 3 to 13. It is now a Church of England Primary School serving Smannell and Enham. Between the school and the church is the distinctive *post box*. *Christ Church, Smannell*, with its decorated brick and flint walls, was designed by the architect W White who also designed Hatherden Church. Both churches were consecrated by the Bishop of Winchester on the same day in November 1857, Smannell at 10.30 am. and Hatherden at 2.30 pm. A fine organ and wall paintings were given in 1890 by the Earle family of Enham Place. The original pews, riddled with woodworm, were recently replaced by oak pews made at the Enham Alamein workshops. The *mother and toddler* next to the *rider* in the bottom corner represent the drug rehabilitation unit

at nearby Ashley Copse. A new mother and baby unit was opened here by the Princess of Wales in 1988, which accounts for the *red helicopter* of the Queen's Flight at the top of the panel.

Lower border

Animals and plants of the countryside; *primroses* and *rabbit*; *blackberries*; *pheasant*; an *oak branch*, representing the village inn, the British Oak.

Little London

White Cottage, Enham Alamein

Candle-making

KNIGHTS ENHAM, ENHAM ALAMEIN

The prefix 'Knights' in the name dates from the 13th century when the manor was in the possession of the Knights Hospitallers, more commonly known as the Knights of St John. 'Alamein' was added after World War II when the people of Egypt presented £225,000 for the building of Alamein Village, and three pairs of wrought-iron gates in gratitude for their deliverance from the Axis powers after the Battle of Alamein in October 1942, which turned the tide of war in favour of the Allies.

Top border

Two books representing Enham's book-binding industry; the *insignia of the Mediterranean Fleet 1942*, the *8th Army* (Desert Rats) and the *Western Desert Air Force* which are featured in the three stained glass windows in the Alamein Church of St George; a *basketful of flowers* representing the combined Enham industries of basket making and the garden centre.

Middle section

The large building at the top of the panel is the *Enham Resource Centre* for assessing the disabled, completed in 1990 and opened by the Patron, H.R.H. the Duchess of Gloucester. The complex, funded entirely by voluntary sources, is the most recent addition to the facilities of Enham Village Centre since its inception just after World War I. The story of the Village Centre began in 1916 when there was concern about the increasing number of men being disabled on the Western Front. A group of people envisaged the creation of a number of Village Centres where such men could find rest, treatment and recuperation as they trained to cope with their disabilities.

In October 1918 Enham Place, a private estate with houses, cottages, buildings and 1,027 acres, was acquired. Exactly a year later Enham Village Centre, planned as the first (but destined to be the only one) of its kind, was officially opened and welcomed the first intake of fifty men.

A medical block had been presented by the British Red Cross Society, and workshops donated by various towns. Training started in horticulture, farming, forestry, woodcraft, poultry rearing, electrical fitting, basket-making, carpentry and joinery, boot and shoe repairing, cookery and rural wood industries, including furniture making.

Within three years more than 1,000 severely disabled ex-servicemen had received training and careful medical attention. In 1926 an old hut, the village entertainment centre was replaced by the Landale Wilson Institute, given by Mr and Mrs D Landale Wilson to mark their silver wedding anniversary.

Enham's workshops played a significant part in Britain's war effort between 1939 and 1945, including the manufacture of glider carcasses. Today, the centre continues to flourish; living accommodation has been improved, while the range of industries has developed and now includes a furniture division and an electronics division. The new Resource Centre includes work, training, education and occupational therapy areas with supporting medical and care facilities, together with Enham's main Occupational Workshop. The *cedar tree* in front of the building is now the logo of the Enham Trust.

The *biplane* in the upper corner symbolises the link between World War I and the manufacture of glider parts in World War II. Below the Resource Centre, on the left, is an *elm tree*, one of many, most of which are now, sadly, lost. The *17th century thatched White Cottage* houses the estate office and a

museum of the Battle of Alamein. *Silver birches* separate this from *St George's, The Alamein Church*, consecrated by the Rt Rev Colin James, Bishop of Basingstoke, on St George's Day 1974. A small private chapel owned by Enham Village Centre, known as St George's Chapel, previously stood on the site. The Alamein Memorial Chapel, which attracts visitors from all over the world, is dedicated to those who took part in the Battle. Below the elm tree is the *bus shelter*, originally a shepherd's hut and rebuilt brick by brick. In front is a *flower stall*, representing the Garden Centre. The building in the centre is *The Landale Wilson Institute*. To its right is the *general store* and *sub-post office*. The disabled are represented by a *lady in a wheelchair and friend*, also emphasising the social aspect provided by the store. In front of the Landale Wilson hall is a *bed of red roses* planted as a memorial to the late Medical Officer Dr MacCullum.

Below the rose garden is *Bradbury House*. Formerly called the White House and used as the village administrative centre, it is now eight flatlets for disabled people. The conservatory has been demolished. In the bottom left corner is the 12th century church of *St Michael, Knights Enham*, depicted with lighted windows to represent its warmth and

constant availability. The *squirrel* in the tree denotes its country setting; a *hedgehog* sits in front. The *imposing gates* in the bottom corner are one of the set of three presented by the Egyptian government. Surrounding the gates are some of the abundant *flora and fauna* including daisies, fly agaric fungus, cuckoo pint, cowslip, bluetits, butterfly and snail. The *poppy* represents the war dead. The huge *candle* made in the workshops is now listed in the Guinness Book of Records. It was 101.7 feet tall and was exhibited at the Andover Show in 1989.

Lower border

Fox, badgers in their sett; *ferns, leaves, robins, ladybird butterflies* and *sheep*.

CHARLTON

There is evidence of Saxon settlement at Charlton but it was only in the 1980s that it achieved recognition as a separate parish, having previously been part of Andover. Nearby Foxcotte, on the other hand, was a thriving little village long before the Conquest with its own chapel. Over the years there was a movement of population from Foxcotte to Charlton, possibly dating from the Black Death.

Top border

Artefacts and a dwelling, representing Charlton's Saxon heritage. During excavations carried out at Old Down Farm in the 1970s evidence of houses of the period was discovered together with various weapons, implements and items of jewellery; the *Charlton Mace Head*: this rare stone mace, dating from somewhere between 5600 to 1800 BC, was found in May 1969 by Mr A F Glover in his garden at Foxcotte Close; the *oak tree* planted to commemorate Queen Victoria's Diamond Jubilee in June 1897; the *bell* presented to the church of St Thomas, Charlton, by Lady Susan Sutton of Penton Lodge on its consecration in March 1908; *symbols representing 'livelihoods'*; a horse shoe

and arable farming; the school, and a baker representing the Hopgood family whose business goes back over 100 years.

Middle section

Just left of centre at the top of the panel is *Marchment Farm*, with grazing sheep, a horse and farm buildings. To the right of the farm is *Foxcotte Tower*. In 1853 Miss Martha Gale (following the example of her uncle Dr Goddard, who had demolished the old church of St Mary, Andover and rebuilt it), pulled down the ancient building of Foxcotte Chapel and rebuilt it. In 1907, with the population of Foxcotte down to 33, the decision was taken to remove the church building from Foxcotte to Charlton but the great opposition dictated that the tower should remain where it was. In the early 1970s it was extended and made into an Arts and Crafts Centre, and in due course it was bought by a London artist for use as an art gallery. It now serves as a play school. The *houses* to the right of the tower represent those built to meet the needs of the area.

The *lake* represents the very popular Charlton Sports and Leisure Centre, built on 76 acres of waste ground. In addition to the boating and fishing lake, sports pavilions

Charlton Sports Centre

and children's play area depicted in the panel, there is also a superb all-weather athletics track and artificial hockey and football pitches. To its left is the thriving *village shop* and post office and across the road is the *church of St Thomas*. This stood at Foxcotte until Dr Frederick Preston, Vicar of Andover from 1902 to 1910, initiated the move to Charlton. Many people felt this was desecration and sacrilegious. Materials from the demolished church were taken in waggons to Charlton. The foundation stone was laid on 3rd March 1908 and consecration, conducted by the Bishop of Dorking, took place on 19th August of the same year.

The *Royal Oak public house* is prominent lower in the panel. It is thought that it began trading as a beer house in 1795 as 'The Three Cups'. In front of the pub is a thriving *flower stall* which was established in the village in 1989 while the *thatched cottages* at the bottom of the panel, located opposite Carters Meadows, are Bluebell Cottage on the left and Snowdrop Cottage on the right. They were once another public house, 'The Buck and Dog'.

Below the splendid *horse-chestnut tree* and *beds of daffodils* are the *watercress beds* which were still being harvested when the panel was designed, but closed in 1993. The site has now been turned into a landscaped private fishing area.

Lower border

Local birds and fish found at Charlton Lakes – *Canada geese*; *moorhens*; *swift, martin* and *swallow*; *trout, chub* and *silver bream*.

Charlton Lakes

Andover

ANDOVER

Andover, the largest town in the Test Valley Borough, has a population of 34,000. At the northern end of the district, it is 18 miles from Romsey and nearly 25 miles from the southern borders.

The unparished area of Andover includes Knights Enham and Enham Alamein. However, those two communities are depicted in a separate Tapestry along with Charlton and Smannell. Accordingly, the boundary line indicates the area covered by the respective Tapestries, and not the parish boundaries.

Andover developed around the crossing point of the River Anton, a tributary of the Test, and was a natural staging point for travellers along the Harroway, a prehistoric trackway, and the Portway, the Roman road running east and west. Small groups settled but all that really survives of those pre-Saxon times is the town's name: from 'Anna-dwfr', or 'Andefera', 'the river of the ash trees'.

When the kingdom of Wessex was established the Kings built their hunting lodges in the vicinity, near excellent hunting forest; traders arrived and the foundations of a prosperous town were laid. It became a chartered borough in 1178 when Henry II granted it the right of a Guild of Merchants. In stage-coaching days it was an important stop on the London-Exeter route, with several inns catering for the traffic, and was sometimes called 'The Gateway to the West'.

Its status as a quiet country market town changed dramatically from 1961 when the Andover Borough Council entered into an agreement with the Greater London Council and Hampshire County Council to move industry and people to Hampshire. New housing developments were planned to cater for a large increase in population, industrial estates were laid out and schools, shops, roads and other amenities followed. Then, under the Local Government Reorganisation of 1974, Andover, with Romsey and Stockbridge, became part of Test Valley District Council (later to become Test Valley Borough Council).

Top border

The *old Norman church* demolished by Dr Goddard in 1841. It replaced a Saxon church on the site, burned down in the great fire of 1141, and was reputed to be the largest and finest example in the country of a church of its kind, a spacious building, covering a much greater area than the present church. The tower had a lead-covered timber spire 80 feet high but this fell in a gale on 11 August 1705. In 1840 the building was lit by gas and had a congregation of 2,000. But Victorian passion for church building led to its destruction, despite the fact that many citizens bitterly resented the demise of their ancient but well loved church. In particular they resented the haphazard way in which fittings were disposed of. The communion table, for example, went to the Angel Inn. A local historian described the demolition of the church as 'an act of terrible vandalism'; the *confirmation of Olaf Tryggvason* by the Bishop of Winchester in Andover in 994. The previous year a Viking army in 94 ships, led by the Norwegian Prince Olaf and the Danish King Swegen, invaded England and attempted, in vain, to sack London. After 'burnings, harryings and killings' along the south coast the Viking forces regrouped for the winter at Southampton.

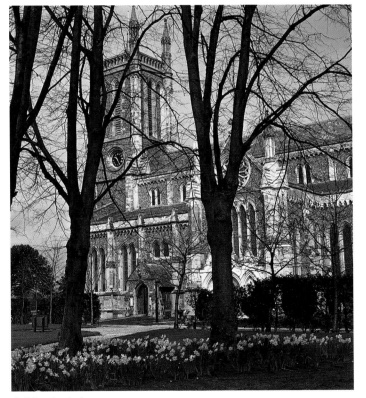

St Mary's, Andover

King Ethelred and his council negotiated with the invaders to supply them with provisions and 16000 pounds of silver in return for a commitment to cease harrying. The King, from his hunting lodge near Andover, sent Alfege, Bishop of Winchester, to bring Olaf to Andover 'with great ceremony'. Olaf, who had previously been converted by a hermit in the Scilly Isles, was confirmed again by the Bishop on the site of St Mary's Church. After the ceremony Ethelred gave Olaf gifts in return for a promise never to return to Britain. Olaf kept his promise and in 995 returned to Norway to convert his new kingdom to Christianity.

A *shepherd and sheep* representing Andover sheep fairs which were not as large as those at nearby Weyhill, but were of considerable local importance; *archery in Common Acre* where men were commanded to prepare for Agincourt. And after Agincourt, in 1542, Henry VIII introduced a form of 'national service' with men being compelled to take part in archery practice at the butts; *'Oliver Twist'* asking for more at Andover workhouse. This refers to the great 'Andover Scandal' of 1846 when a Parliamentary Select Committee probed the running of the workhouse under ex-Sergeant Major McDougal and his wife. The union work-

Brewer's dray at Town Mills

house in Junction Road was built in 1836 and McDougal, who had fought at Waterloo, and his wife were appointed as Master and Matron. The Board of Guardians set the inmates to grinding bones for fertiliser. The McDougals were dishonest and cruel had provided so poor a diet that inmates gnawed the bones for the marrow. A young London reporter, Charles Dickens, had covered similar inquiries for his paper and the idea of the Oliver Twist plot was conceived; the *Norman arch* which formed the west door of the old church was taken down and rebuilt on another site in the High Street. It is now known as 'Norman Gate'; a *bullock* representing the old cattle markets.

Middle section

The buildings in the middle of the panel on the left are the *Town Mills*. At the time of Domesday there were six mills in Andover. One of them, the Town Mill, in the centre of the complex, still straddles the river and is now a restaurant and public house. The main building in the panel is *the Guildhall*. There has been a Guildhall at the northern end of the High Street market place for centuries for the meetings of the town's governing bodies. One such building stood there from 1583 to 1724 and another from 1725 to 1825. The present Guildhall, constructed in Bath stone to the plans of John Harris, was built in 1825/26 at a cost of around £9,000. Furnishing it cost a further £600 and on 6 June 1826 the Corporation moved into the new Council Chamber. The Guildhall had two floors, the lower one open and arched for use by stallholders as a covered market.

Originally the building had a clock turret but that was removed in 1904. There were three flagpoles, one for the union flag, one for the Lord Lieutenant and one for the Borough. The *gas lamp standard* in the forecourt was erected to commemorate the Diamond Jubilee of Queen Victoria in 1897. Later consigned to a Council yard it was

re-erected in 1977 to mark the Queen's Silver Jubilee. The Guildhall was refurbished in 1981.

Dominating the right hand side of the panel, as it does the town, is *St Mary's Church*, seen from Marlborough Street. The church was built by Dr William Stanley Goddard, Headmaster of Winchester College from 1793 to his retirement in 1809. He married an Andover heiress, Henrietta Gale. In 1835 the Vicar, the Rev Charles Ridding, and Dr Goddard decided that the church was too small for 'this agreeable little town' and that possibly the tower was unsafe. After Henrietta's death in 1830 Dr Goddard used his inherited wealth for local charitable purposes and he agreed to be the 'anonymous' benefactor for a new church. Plans were drawn up by a young architect Augustus Livesay whose design, in Victorian Gothic, was modelled on Salisbury Cathedral. The estimated cost was £9,437. The church was built of Caen stone shipped in by the Andover canal for a start in 1841. Work went well until 3rd June 1842 when the roof fell in causing the death of one workman. Two days later the south clerestory wall collapsed. Many Andoverians who resented the loss of the old church saw those incidents as evidence of divine disfavour.

Town Mills

St John's, formerly the Workhouse

Andover Guildhall at Christmas

Andover on market day

The first Divine Service in the new St Mary's was held on Sunday, 11th August 1844. The final demolition of the old church and the completion of the tower took until 1846 by which time the cost had risen to more than £20,000, well over double the original estimate. Sadly, Dr Goddard did not live to see the completion of his church, as he died on 10 October, 1845. Sir Nicholas Pevsner describes it as a 'very remarkable building' and the design 'extraordinary and quite brilliant'.

The large building below and to the right of the church is *Keens House*, in the old Town Station Yard, the original headquarters of the TSB Trust Company, which moved from London to Andover in 1973. As the work-force increased to more than 1500 it became Andover's largest employer and it supports the community in many ways. TSB Trust Company, subsequently renamed TSB Bank plc, expanded to occupy new offices in Charlton Place in 1986.

The imposing building in the bottom left corner is the listed *Savoy Chambers* in London Street which has been virtually rebuilt. Originally the Star and Garter inn it was first built in the 18th Century, and acquired in 1770 by the enterprising Heath

family to become a focus for brewing and banking. In 1861 it was sold to Dr Jabez Elliott, a surgeon, who named it Elliott House. In 1934 it became Savoy Chambers and has been used by various local companies for office accommodation. The houses next to it are situated at the top of *Chantry Street*.

Centre bottom is the so-called *Round House*, one of the two tollhouses which served Andover. One was at the junction of Salisbury Road and Weyhill Road and the other at the Tavern crossroads for the collection of tolls from users of the turnpike roads. On the right of the Round House is the former Workhouse *St John's Hospital*, built in 1836 and still serving as an old peoples' unit when the Andover panel was designed. The building is now part of the Cricklade College complex, with a teaching block, tutorial rooms and the teachers' centre. The long building in the bottom corner is the *War Memorial Hospital* in Charlton Road. After the Great War in 1918 a new hospital was proposed and a committee chaired by Dr E A Farr, Medical Officer of Health for Andover, was set up to raise the estimated cost of £16,000. The first town Carnival in 1924 brought in £1,300 and soon the total amount, a considerable sum in the twenties, was raised.

Work began in 1925. The War Memorial
Hospital was opened on 30th June 1926 by
Field Marshal the Viscount Allenby. The
first name in the Visitors' Book is that of
H.R.H. Edward, Prince of Wales, later King
Edward VIII. He combined a visit to the
hospital with an engagement the previous
day when he had opened the Landale
Wilson Institute in Enham Village Centre.

Lower border

*Wild dog rose; grebe; daffodil; fox; ducks; poppy;
badger; wild arum; owl; toadstools; hedgehog;
brimstone butterfly; violet; chalk hill blue
butterfly; viper or adder.*

View towards Andover

Thruxton
Fyfield
Kimpton

THRUXTON, FYFIELD and KIMPTON

© Crown copyright licence no. LA079715

These three villages lie in a triangle within a mile or so from each other just north of the busy A303 to the west.

THRUXTON

Five miles from Andover, Thruxton was almost certainly one of four 'Annes' named in the Domesday Book under the Andover Hundred. In the 12th century the name was Turkilleston which, over the centuries, changed via Thruckleston (16th century), Throxton (18th century) to the present form. Gliders flew to Arnhem from the World War II airfield to the west of the village. Now Thruxton is nationally known as a motor racing centre. Unlike the racing circuit, the village can hardly be seen from the main road. In 1985 the centre of the village was declared a Conservation Area.

Top border

Racing car, representing the Thruxton Racing Circuit, which opened on the airfield in March 1968 and is the home of racing run by the British Automobile Racing Club; *arms of Lisle impailing Courtenay*. Sir John Lisle who died in 1407 is buried in the churchyard. His magnificent brass in the

church, one of the best examples of the earliest type of joined chain mail armour, carries his own arms with those of his wife, Elizabeth. His feet rest on a lion and part of the brass is depicted in the lower border; *carrier's cart* of Mr E Piper. Mr Piper lived at Flint House and operated as the village carrier with his wagonette and horse, taking goods and passengers between Thruxton, Andover and Salisbury. Behind the wagon is one of the *buses* of the Amport and district Bus Company which now provides local services.

Middle section

In the top left hand corner is the *parish church of St Peter and St Paul*, tucked away off School Lane beside the manor house. Parts date from the 13th and 15th centuries but most of the present church dates from a 19th century restoration. Its treasures are the tombs and effigies of some of the lords and ladies of the manor, especially two 13th century coffin slabs and a 17th century wooden effigy of Elizabeth Philpott, lady of the manor, who was buried in 1616. Sadly, it is badly battered but her fashionable clothes are beautifully carved. Not visible to the public is the oldest bell, given in 1581, which was rung to warn of the coming Armada.

The original manor was destroyed and no trace remains but the *present manor*, built probably in the first half of the 18th century, is featured below the church. In front of the house is a fine *horse chestnut tree*. In the centre is another fine tree, a *sycamore*, planted by the Rev H D Baker to commemorate the birth of his son. At its foot is an old *milestone* which was moved to the village from the A303, the old turnpike road. The inscription gives the mileage to London as LXVIIII (69), not the normal LXIX, and to Andover V (5).

Inside the thatched wall in the centre, dating from the 17th century, is *Manor Cottage*, with the four windows. The white building behind Manor Cottage is the *Rectory* which was completed in 1837 by the Rev Donald Baynes. He also built the school in 1836, and each day boys would go to draw water from the pump room in the Rectory for the school. The Rectory was also the home of Dorothy Kerin, a faith healer of renown, who lived with the Rev Langford James in the early 1920s.

The *blue cottage*, a former cobbler's shop from which a Mr Scrivens sold pots and pans, was restored in the early 1970s since when it has been a very attractive feature of the village. Next to it is *Bray Cottage*, formerly the village bakery and general stores. The Bray family were bakers in Thruxton until 1969 and their excellent bread was delivered over a wide area. The thatched roof was destroyed by fire in 1985. At the top of the panel are *Robins Roost and Forge Cottage* built in the 17th century of chalk and flint. In the past Robins Roost served the village as a laundry while the adjacent Forge Cottage was formerly known as School Cottage until the blacksmith's son, Ernest Lansley, took over his father's business and moved to Forge Cottage where horses were shod and wooden wheels were bound.

Lower border

This depicts the famous *snowdrops* and *primroses* which are a special feature of the village; the *name Turkilleston*. Turkil was a Saxon who had a 'tun', the Saxon word for 'farmstead' and later a hamlet or village. In the centre is part of the *brass of Sir John Lisle* in the parish church.

Aerial view of Thruxton airfield and circuit

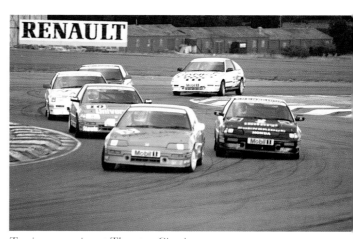

Touring car racing at Thruxton Circuit

45

FYFIELD

The parish of Fyfield, which includes Redenham, is situated a few miles west of Andover, near the Wiltshire border. It was once a mere handful of thatched cottages with three large houses, the Manor, the Grange and the Rectory.

Top border

Section of the Roman pavement excavated in the 19th century and now in the British Museum. As can be seen, it incorporates a reference to the local family of Bodeni.

Toby Balding's racing yard at Fyfield

The excavations were carried out on Lambourne's Hill where other finds included a Roman hypocaust and pottery in 1830 and a range of four rooms in 1850; *arms of William Maudit* who held the manor, reduced to 3 hides, from 1086; *Rev Henry White*, former Rector of Fyfield, with his pitchpipe. His brother, the celebrated naturalist Gilbert White, wrote to his friend Daines Barrington from Fyfield on 12 February, 1771: 'My musical friend (i.e. his brother Henry) at whose house I am now visiting has tried all the owls that are in his near neighbourhood with a pitchpipe set at concert pitch and finds that they all hoot in B flat'; *the tug-of-war* across the Pillhill Brook between teams from Fyfield and Kimpton as part of the celebrations marking the Queen's Silver Jubilee in 1977.

Middle section

In the centre is the *Church of England School*, attended by pupils from all three villages. A plaque records the official opening: 'Dedicated by Faulkner Alison, Lord Bishop of Winchester, 21st September, 1966. Replaces Church of England schools in Fyfield, Thruxton and Kimpton which were founded in 1818, 1836 and 1872'. It was built to accommodate 70 pupils but two extra classrooms have since been added. *The child skipping* in front of the school is Karen, the grand daughter of Mrs Kathleen Pennells who embroidered this piece and who used strands of Karen's own hair for the hair in the tapestry. Also near the school is the *old school bell* from the former Fyfield National School, now a private residence, 'Bell Cottage'.

At the top the name of the village is shown on a *banner being towed by a plane*. Recording that planes carrying advertising banners often took off from Thruxton airfield and flew over the area. On the left is the *village post box* and the traditional *red telephone kiosk* which was there when the panel was worked but has since been replaced by steel and glass.

On *Walnut Tree Green* to the right, is the *village shop* and a representative *new house*. The magnificent display of *daffodils* were bought with village funds and planted by children in 1983.

Fyfield is known throughout the racing world as the home of G B (Toby) Balding, the racehorse trainer with two Grand National and many other wins to his credit. The *string of racehorses* represents those seen at exercise through the village in early mornings. His Grand National winners were Highland Wedding in 1969 and Little Polvier in 1989. The *pub sign* was changed to *Highland Wedding* to commemorate the victory. The small *church of St Nicholas* lies out of sight of the village street, down a lane next to the Manor. It dates from the 13th century but, like so many others, was extensively 'restored' by Victorian enthusiasts. Both pitchpiping Rev Henry White and his wife are buried in the churchyard. There is a *memorial oak tree* to Brigadier Simpson.

Bottom right hand is *Littleton Manor*. Littleton was once a separate village and at the time of Domesday was larger than either Fyfield or Kimpton but all that now remains are the Manor and Forge Cottage, home of Gillian Yarde-Leavett, one of the panel's designers. The other manor, Redenham, is represented by their *green village pump* seen above the church.

Lower border

Racehorse; a *heron*; some *ducks* and *geese* in front of Littleton.

Parish church, Kimpton

KIMPTON

Kimpton, source of the Pillhill Brook, six miles west of Andover, is a picturesque village with a number of thatched cottages, and even a thatched bus shelter. The main part of the village is clustered around the green while the other end had the school, now demolished, and now the village hall. It is known for the discovery at Karlis corner in 1966, by local archaeologist Max Dacre, of a Bronze Age cemetery. The farmer, William Flambert, cooperated by leaving part of the field uncultivated for four years during the extensive 'dig'. The archaeologists found evidence of 108 cremation burials in pottery urns up to 3500 years old to about 800 BC. All the finds are now in the British Museum.

Top border

The *other half of the Silver Jubilee tug-of-war* featured in the Fyfield panel, with the difference that the end of the Kimpton rope is looped round a tree!; the *crossed keys of St Peter and St Paul*, representing the parish church; *memorial on the north wall of the church to Robert Thornburgh* who died in 1522. Above the tomb which is half buried in the wall are two tablets. The lower one invites prayers for the souls of Robert and his wives and children. Above it is a brass relief of Robert in armour followed by brasses of his first wife and her two children and his second wife and her seven children; *urns* representing the excavations at Karlis Corner.

Middle section

At the top of the panel is a *field of stubble* after harvest at Poplar Farm. In the centre is *Garden Cottage*, one of the thatched houses which give such charm to the village, and, top right, the *Little Stranger* public house, formerly the New Inn. In the centre on the left is the *old thatched barn*, now a private residence, and on the right, on the green, the *thatched bus shelter*. Nearby, walking her dog Dolly, is *Mrs Gertie Coster*, a familiar figure when the panel was worked but, sadly, no longer living. Above her is the old *cast iron village pump*. The *signpost* at the road junction is also of cast iron. Above the sign post and the bus shelter is another thatched cottage, *Kimpton Cottage*.

Prominent is the *parish church of St Peter and St Paul*, situated behind Kimpton Manor and reached via a grass path. The present church was built in stages over a century and a half, from 1220 to 1370. It has had restorations but apart from the tower, no major structural alterations and it is therefore unified and harmonious. The original tower had become dangerous and was rebuilt between 1837 and 1839. The altar in the Shoddesden chapel on the north side of the church is the village war memorial. The small *daphne tree* depicted in the panel in the churchyard was planted in memory of Daphne Norman (nee Wise) who died at the age of 23 in 1982. The fine *copper beech tree* stands at the entrance to the churchyard.

To the right of the church is *Kimpton Manor*, previously the Rectory. A century ago the Rector moved out to a new Rectory built on higher ground as he suspected that there could well be drainage problems there. In 1995 he was proved right as, in the worst floods in living memory, a number of people have had to have their drains pumped out. An interesting feature of the Manor House is that the Deeds stipulate that wild bees in the end wall must be preserved. The *weeping willow* outside the manor was planted by Mrs Joan Pool in memory of her son Anthony who was killed in 1969 while hunting. Sadly, the tree was blown down during the great gale of 1987. In the bottom righthand corner is a fine *horse chestnut tree* with a *cow and calf* grazing by the Pillhill Brook.

Lower border

Some of the *cattle and sheep* on local farms and the family of *black kittens* which roamed Manor Farm Yard when the tapestry was being planned.

Wild flowers by Pillhill Brook

Weyhill
Shipton Bellinger
Tidworth

WEYHILL, SHIPTON BELLINGER and TIDWORTH

© Crown copyright licence no. LA079715

WEYHILL

For nine centuries until the 1950s, Weyhill was the venue of one of the most celebrated country fairs in Britain. The site was at the crossroads of two ancient trading routes, one from Cornwall to Kent (The Harrow Way) along which Cornish tin was carried, and the other ('the Gold Road') from Holyhead to Christchurch Bay, along which Irish gold was brought for shipping to the continent.

Originally held on Old Michaelmas Day and lasting for about a week, the fair was renowned for its enormous sales of sheep and hops. In its heyday horses, cheese and leather were also sold. It served as a hiring fair for servants and farm labourers and inevitably took on the nature of a pleasure fair. In Thomas Hardy's 'The Mayor of Casterbridge' Weyhill Fair became Weydon Priors where Henchard sold his wife and child for five guineas.

Now, with the demise of the fair, Weyhill is a quiet place three miles from Andover, bypassed by the main trunk road to the west.

Top border

Shows items associated with the fair: *The Weyhill Ghost*: folklore has it that a west country hop merchant named Leadbetter, arriving late at the Star Inn, was allocated the ostler's room. He was awakened by a noise on the stairs and saw a tall, gaunt figure with a candle in one hand and a butcher's knife in the other. The figure approached the bed, shook Leadbetter by the shoulders and drew the knife several times across his throat. He put the light on the table and left. Later in the night the awesome visitor returned with the knife, smeared with blood.

Terrified, Leadbetter fled and stammered his story to the landlord. But the ostler arrived to reveal the apparition was a deaf and dumb man who had been given orders to wake him at 4 o'clock to remind him that he had a pig to kill. A popular ballad, about 'The Weyhill Ghost' had a wide circulation; *sheep bells*, symbolising the sheep fair; *'horning the colt'* an ancient ceremony held at The Star and other locations. A newcomer to the fair, a 'colt', was initiated by the 'horning' rite. He was seated and a hat surmounted with two horns between which was fixed a cup, was placed on his head. Various verses with the chorus 'Horns, boys, horns; horns, boys, horns, and drink like his daddy, with a large pair of horns', were then sung while the cup was filled with ale which the colt had to drink, afterwards paying for half a gallon of ale for the assembled company; *hops and cheeses* sold at the fair.

Middle section

The *church of St Michael* is in the top left corner. A church at Weyhill is mentioned in the Domesday Book but the oldest part of the present church, the chancel arch, dates from the end of the 12th century. In 1506 ten oaks were sold from Ramridge wood for 8s 4d for roof repairs while in 1822 the lead on the roof was sold (over 3 tons for £64) and replaced by Welsh slates. The church was largely restored in the middle of the 19th century. The base of the cross in the church-yard is 13th century but the cross itself was brought from Jerusalem and added in 1904.

Weyhill Lodge to the right of the church has been converted into luxury flats. In the corner is part of the *yard and a crane* of A J Dunning and Son (Weyhill) Ltd on the old fairground site. The building firm was started in Penton by Alfred James Dunning in 1917, his son Victor being in the business from the

Mural at the Weyhill Fair inn

Detail - Sheep Fair and old Sun Inn

very beginning. The firm's premises moved to the site of the old sheep fair in 1921 and the business flourished establishing an enviable reputation in the diverse fields of property development, construction work, shopfitting, scaffolding over a very wide area and, more locally in undertaking and farming. It became a limited company in 1936. In post-war years, Dunnings played its part in the redevelopment of Andover. It was, however, a victim of the recession, going into receivership in December 1989. Parts of the firm still continue under a new name, and at Weyhill Farm.

The *houses below the church* include council houses, Barrett homes and an old folk's bungalow. The *thatched building* across the road, originally two cottages, is now a farm house. The *horse and rider* going over the jump in the centre are a reminder of the riding stables run by Mrs Hartigen at Homestead, now a nursing home. Horse trials and point to point races were held locally. The *row of cottages* below the rider are owned by the Parish Council and were originally for the poor of the parish but are now let. Across the road is *Ramridge House* on whose land the greater part of Weyhill Fair was once held. For years it was used as a furniture store for Dunnings but was later

sold for conversion to flats. The *cows* in the bottom right corner represent local mixed farming, while in the opposite corner is the *village pond* with swan, mallard, coot and moorhen. The swan was used for the badge of the *village school* featured at the bottom of the panel. Built as a National School in 1855, with Miss Julia Hall as the Mistress, it was supported by public subscriptions and the 'children's pence'. Its one room was rather dark, with whitewashed walls but in 1897 the school was enlarged to accommodate 80 children. Sadly, because of falling numbers of children, it was forced to close in 1988.

Lower border

Catkins; *primroses, robin*; *hawthorn berries*; *hazel nuts*; *snowdrops*; *mushroom*; *deer* and *heron*.

St Michael's, Weyhill

SHIPTON BELLINGER

Inhabitants of Shipton Bellinger eked out a living for centuries on poor soil, barely six inches above the chalk in places; with little fertile farmland, sheep farming was the major livelihood and the village name comes from the Saxon 'Sceap Tun', or sheep farm. The parish, on the eastern edge of Salisbury Plain, is like a finger of Hampshire poked into Wiltshire. It was only when the Army came to Tidworth that the village began to develop as a dormitory area for the garrison. It is now a mixture of old and new.

At Domesday the village was recorded as Sceptone and Snodingstone, the two manors. The Bellinger connection was added in 1297 when Ingram Berenger became Lord of the Manor of Shipton.

Top border

The *three medieval bells of St Peter's Church* which have probably been rung since at least the late 16th century. All three are listed for preservation by the Council for the Care of Churches. The treble bell has the inscription 'Johannes Cristi care dignare pro bois orare' (John, beloved of Christ, deign to pray for us). The second is inscribed 'God be our Guyd

RB 1600'. The largest, the tenor, over three feet in diameter and weighing 9 cwt, is inscribed 'Sancte Nicolae ora pro nobis' (Saint Nicholas pray for us); the *mail coach* which ran daily from Marlborough to Salisbury in the early 19th century. It arrived at The Boot Inn with mail at 6.30 in the morning and returned at 6.30 in the evening; the *Ram* is the village symbol; *sign of The Boot*, the village inn.

Middle section

St Peter's Church is prominent at the top. There is evidence of a 10th century church in the village, although it is unlikely that anything remains. The present stone and flint church, with its stone windows and a wooden bell turret, was at least partly built in the 14th century and may have been restored three hundred years later. There was a well documented major restoration in 1879 at a cost of £1500, but there is a mystery regarding the churchyard. Contemporary reports reveal that the Churchwardens, Messrs Gilbert and Rumsey, 'lowered the Churchyard in some places as much as four or five feet', at their own expense. Churchwarden's accounts, however, show that money was paid from Church Funds for 71½ days' work in the churchyard.

The *village sign* was erected by the Parish Council in 1982, the date being added to the shield of the Berenger family, but when the sign was repainted the date was left out. The *sheep* reflect the age old tradition of sheep farming.

The *thatched cottage* on the left is Bramble Cottage in the High Street, the oldest house in the village and a listed building. Below it is the village's ivy-covered *post box*. The imposing house at the bottom of the panel is *Manor Farm House* the only one of the five village farms left. The rear of the building is old but the front is Victorian. The *pheasant* flying over the village is a reminder of local field sports practised in the north of the parish by the Officers' Shoot and in the south by Snoddington Manor Estate.

Lower border

Hedgehog; *purple milk vetch* (Astragalus Damcus) rare in Southern England; *lapwing*; *short-eared owl* (found on the Plain); *red admiral butterfly*; *primroses*.

Garrison Church at Tidworth

Piper of the 2nd Tank Regiment, Tidworth

TIDWORTH

When the Test Valley Tapestry was being worked the garrison town of Tidworth sat astride the Wiltshire border and the county boundary divided the town with only half, South Tidworth, being in Hampshire. Some buildings had their fronts in South Tidworth (Hants) and their backs in North Tidworth (Wilts). Now the whole of Tidworth is within Wiltshire following a review of local government boundaries.

Tidworth and its surrounding countryside has been a training ground for the British Army since 1902 when 42,000 acres were bought, including the Tedworth Estate, once the home of Thomas Assheton-Smith, a celebrated huntsman. Tidworth House, built in 1828-30 with its gracious grounds is now the splendid officers' club and nursing sisters' quarters, next to the arena where polo is played and the famous Tidworth Tattoo was staged until 1977.

At the time of Domesday Tedorde or Todeorde comprised North and South Tedworth, each with about 30 people and each containing three separate manors.

Upper border

Nuns' Walk and Nuns' Market. In 1164 Henry II granted the tithes of North and South Tidworth to the nuns of Amesbury and a charter for a weekly market. The nuns walked to Tidworth, giving rise to the name Nuns' Walk; the *Tedworth Drummer Boy*: in March 1661 William Drury, a Tidworth drummer, tried to obtain money in Ludgershall by subterfuge, using 'a counterfeit pass and warrant'. John Mompesson, the magistrate, confiscated his drum which was eventually sent to Mompesson's home, Tedworth House. Soon phantom drums rattled, loud scratching sounds were heard and 'there was violent beating and shaking of bedsteads'. These disturbances led to the first recorded poltergeist investigation when King Charles II sent his chaplain, the Rev. Joseph Glanvil, an authority on witchcraft, to investigate. He was unable to determine positively whether or not trickery was involved; a *mounted soldier* representing cavalry regiments associated with Tidworth; a *modern tank* and *helicopter*.

Middle section

Top left is *The Tower* or Observatory, built by the squire, Thomas Assheton-Smith so that his disabled daughter could watch the hunt. But it also had a further potential use. He had a barrel of tar installed on top of the tower to be lit if information was received of the approach of rioters bent on wrecking agricultural machinery. To the right of the tower is the little *Burial Chapel* in the woods, built using some of the material from the old South Tedworth Church which was demolished in 1784. The chapel was the only local place of worship until the church of St Mary the Virgin was built in 1880. It became very dilapidated but thanks to a generous legacy it has now been restored and is used for a monthly 'Songs of Praise' service and the occasional baptism.

Prominent at the top of the panel is *Tedworth House* built in 1828, when a former house on the site was demolished, and completed in 1830. The small house in the fork of the road is *the White Lodge*, built at the entrance to the drive of the big house and still occupied today. The red brick building to the left of the Lodge was the *Church of England School* endowed by Mrs Assheton-Smith in 1857. She 'clothed 16 scholars . . .

the sight of the girls in their red cloaks on a Saturday afternoon and of the noisy urchins rushing from the porch would suffice to gladden the heart'. The school was enlarged in 1903 to provide accommodation for 110 pupils but it was demolished in 1985 despite local attempts to have it preserved for a museum. There are now six schools serving the Tidworth area. The *red house* further up the road represents the station houses while to the right are *thatched cottages* by the old Reading Room on the border of North and South Tidworth. The *Reading Room* itself is alongside, in front of which is one of the old style *red telephone kiosks*.

The *factory type building* in the centre is the Royal Ordnance Depot which issues clothing and equipment to Army personnel. In front of the Depot is the *Royal British Legion Club* built on the site of an old cinema which was burnt down. Across the road is a *garage* which has subsequently been rebuilt as a modern petrol filling station.

Below the garage is the parish *Church of The Holy Trinity*. This 13th century building served North Tidworth but when the South Tidworth church was made redundant it became the parish church for the whole town. It is part of the United Benefice of

Tidworth, Ludgershall and Faberstown. Below the British Legion Club are two *cottages in Pennings Road*, the only two of a line left standing, while further down the road, in the left bottom corner, is the *Ram Inn*, the third of the same name on the same site. Opposite is a former *grocery shop and a post office*. Both have been demolished to make way for a new fish and chip shop and restaurant.

Lower border

Butterflies; *badger*; *sheep*; *hares and rabbits*; *squirrel*; *owl*; *pheasant*; *fox*; *hawthorn and blackberry bushes*; *corn field*; *the Tedworth Hunt*.

Monxton
Amport
Grateley

MONXTON, AMPORT and GRATELEY

© Crown copyright licence no. LA079715

Monxton village street

MONXTON

Monxton, with its attractive thatched cottages, is a long, narrow village spread along both sides of the Pillhill Brook. Its neighbours along the line of the brook are Amport to the west and Abbotts Ann and Anna Valley to the east.

Top border

The *arms of King's College Cambridge*. The manor of Monxton was included in the property that Henry VI granted to the college (originally the Royal College of the Blessed Mary and St Nicholas) when he founded it in 1441. There are many records of 'Monkestone' in the muniment room at King's; *Bec 1094 AD*. After the Conquest in 1066 the manor was granted to Hugh de Grandmesnil, a Norman baron, who then granted it to the Abbey of Bec-Hellouin in Normandy. The abbey held 'Anne de Bec', as it was then called, for the next 300 years. In 1404 Henry IV gave it to to his son John of Lancaster, constable of England, and when John died in 1435 it passed to Henry VI; *1920s*: King's college continued to be the corporate lord of the manor of Monxton

and to own much property in the village until 1921 when it sold the properties under the hammer at auction.

Middle section

At the top is the *parish church of St Mary*. This was rebuilt in 1853-54 in brick and flint on the site of the medieval parish church, of which only the 12th century capitals of the chancel arch remain. There is a fine brass in the floor of the nave of a kneeling lady in Elizabethan dress with a man, also kneeling, behind her. The parson from 1723 to 1748 was Thomas Rothwell who was so devoted to mathematics that he would sit alone in his parlour to which not even members of his family were admitted. Occupying himself 'with figures and Algebra . . . that for many of the last years of his life he stirred not out of his house, no, not even to Church, but had a constant Curate . . . and gave himself not time to be shaved, but let his beard grow till he was a spectacle . . .' Flying near the church are *doves from the dovecot* on the right, from the forecourt of Monxton Manor. The row of *thatched cottages* along the village street are probably 17th century. At the end is the *Black Swan Inn* (commonly known as the Mucky Duck), which has been the village pub at least since the 17th century. The *old water pump* stands above one of the old village wells in the front garden of Well Cottage. The house on the other side of the road, with the large window, is *Hutchens Cottage*, formerly a farmhouse.

The *wall with the mill wheel* built into it is outside Monxton Mill. There was a mill here in 1086, worth 7s 6d at the time. *The bridge* is at the other end of the village over the Pillhill Brook which rises in Kimpton and then flows through Amport and Monxton before joining the River Anton near Upper Clatford. *A magpie* sits on the bridge. Also in the centre section are *Canada geese*, *kingfisher* and *local plants*, *leaves* and *flowers – lily*, *foxglove*, *lords and ladies*, *bullrushes* and *greater bladder-wort*.

Lower border

Duck; *swan*; *water iris*; *frog, dragonfly*; *heron*.

Monxton Cottages

Thatching

View along Pillhill Brook, East Cholderton

Stained glass window in Amport church

AMPORT

Amport is an irregular-shaped village in the valley of the Pillhill Brook, four miles west of Andover. It was called Anna in the Domesday Book; the source of this name may be Saxon ('ashtree') or possibly Celtic ('brook'). When William the Conqueror gave the manor to Hugh de Port it became Anne de Port which over the years changed to Amport.

Top border

The *badge of the RAF Chaplain's Department,* based in Amport House; *part of the coat of arms of the Sheppard/Routh family.* In 1801 Dr Thomas Sheppard, whose father was the wealthy Rector of Basingstoke, married Sophia Routh, a daughter of the Revd Peter Routh of Beccles and a woman with a keen social conscience. Thomas inherited substantial property in Amport from his father, a curate there, and when Thomas died it passed to Sophia. Thomas's Will stipulated that she should spend at least two months every year in Amport but she built a house and lived there for the rest of her long life, using her wealth for philanthropic purposes. In 1815 she built and endowed the school and six almshouses; *the symbol of the Paulets* who were prominent in the village

for generations. In 1649 Lord Henry Powlett purchased the manor of Amport. His great-great-grandson Charles who began rebuilding Amport House, which was completed in 1806, also changed the spelling of the family name from Powlett to Paulet, as the senior branch of the family had long done. As the 13th Marquis of Winchester he extended the estate to over 2000 acres; *motto of the almshouses 'for six poor widows AD 1815';* another *part of the Sheppard Routh coat of arms.*

Middle section

At the top of the panel is *Amport House,* built by the 14th Marquis of Winchester in 1857 on the site of the mansion built by his father fifty years earlier. He demolished the farm buildings and cottages there, replacing them with extensive kitchen gardens, glass houses and orchards, putting up new cottages for his workers, and farm buildings half a mile away. During the time of the 16th Marquis (who died in 1962 aged one hundred), King Edward VII and Lily Langtry stayed at Amport House for the Stockbridge races and partridge shooting. The property is listed and has a garden designed by Gertrude Jeckyll. Amport House was requisitioned by the RAF in September 1939 and eventually bought by the Air Ministry to become the RAF Chaplains School. To the left is the *cricket field*.

On the right of the house is the *parish church of St Mary*, originally built about 1320-1330. In 1866 the church was restored with a rebuilt north transept, new north and south windows and the porch and vestry.

In the centre typical *Amport cottages* lead up to the *school*, which has served the village well for 180 years. The scene of Amport School pupils dancing round the *maypole on the green* is one of the most delightful features in the whole Tapestry. The green is used for the school's Dance Festival held every year on 12th May, continuing a tradition started by Mrs Sheppard. She had a maypole erected in her garden and invited all the children from the school to dance around it, giving them a penny and a currant bun. The celebration was held on Old May Day, 12th May instead of 1st May, and so it is to this day. By the *red telephone kiosk* opposite the school is the well-known figure of *Mrs Mac and her dog*.

In the bottom righthand corner is the *window of Grateley School* which could not be squeezed into the Grateley panel. This 'overlapping' is an example of happy

co-operation between the designers and the embroiderers of the two panels. The *flora and fauna* around the green are typical of those seen in the village. *Snowdrops* cover the church grounds in the Spring.

Lower border

Violets; *hazelnuts*; *ladybirds*; *primroses*; *holly and berries*; *grasses*, *hedgehog* and *roses* – all to be seen in abundance along the lanes.

St Mary's Church, Amport

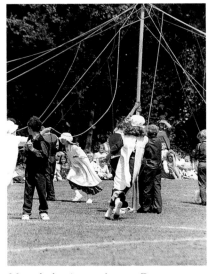
Maypole dancing at Amport Green

St Leonard's, Grateley

The Plough Inn, Grateley

GRATELEY

Grateley in the north west corner of Hampshire derives its name from the 'greatnlea' or 'big wood clearing' to the southwest of the church. It is a village split into two distinct parts, one clustered around the church, Manor Farm and the Plough Inn, and the other a mile away around the railway built in the late 19th century.

Top border

The legend along the top of the border *'Laws for All England 925'*, refers to the council (or witanagemot) which the Saxon King Athelstan, self-styled 'King of the English' is reputed to have held here in 925, drawing up the first Code of Laws for all England. His enactments provided for a uniform coinage and dealt with the punishment of thieves. *Quarley's three historic church bells* are housed in a roofed, ground-floor frame alongside the church wall and are rung by hand from inside the church; *motifs* from some of the very old floor tiles, possibly from Clarendon Palace, now in the chancel of the church; the *shield* is from the coat of arms of the Maudit family, the first

prominent land-owners in Grateley in the 12th century; the *chain* is the symbol of St Leonard, patron saint of prisoners.

Middle section

Top left is *Quarley Hill*, site of an Iron Age fort, which overlooks the village. It is the only hill fort in Hampshire which has four entrances at opposite points, after the fashion of Roman camps and it could well have been here that Athelstan held his council. Below Quarley Hill are *commercial chicken houses* representing several hatcheries in the village. A *train* stands at *Grateley station*, now just a halt. When the railway was built the powerful Boutcher family did not relish the idea of having a station near their house in the village – so it was built a mile away. The road joining the two parts of the village was once a private road connecting the Boutcher's Grateley House to the station. Above the station is a *helicopter* on exercise from Middle Wallop.

Below the chicken houses is *St Leonard's Church*. The nave is mainly 12th century. The 13th century stained glass in one of the panels of the east window was 'rescued' from a restoration of Salisbury cathedral by the architect James Wyatt. He had thrown it in a ditch where it was spotted, retrieved and taken to Grateley.

Below the station are *postwar houses* while the *barn and grain silo* are at Manor Farm. The imposing *Plough Inn* in the centre of the village is featured on the centre right, with its fine specimen of a *horse-chestnut tree*, one of several planted to commemorate the Diamond Jubilee in 1897. Another, with pink 'candles', is in the bottom right-hand corner. *Swallows* perch on the wire above the *village store and post office*, on the right of which is *Hope Cottage*. Walking their dogs past the two cottages are *Mrs Harman and Mrs Holland*, familiar figures when the panel was being worked. *Farmer Peter Clarke* is seen in the bottom right-hand corner with one of his *shire horses*, a feature of the village – the public house near the station, formerly the Railway Hotel, is now called the Shire Horse. *Aylesbury ducks* swim on the pond while *yellow flag irises* and *lords and ladies* grow on the bank and *holly blue butterflies* flutter above. In the bottom left-hand corner is the entrance and doorway of *Grateley School*, with part of the building in the Amport panel. The school has served the village for generations.

Lower border

Brambles; a *deer*; *fungi*; *oak leaves*; *pheasants* and a *harvest mouse*.

Quarley Hill in winter

The church bells at Quarley

Abbotts Ann
Little Ann

LITTLE ANN   ABBOTTS ANN

ABBOTTS ANN and LITTLE ANN

© Crown copyright licence no. LA079715

This panel is unlike any other, both in design and detail. Its designer, retired Group Captain Alan Selby, a Council colleague of Laurie Porter, lived in the village from 1951 until a year before his death in 1990. Unable to achieve the standards he sought on the proposed canvas, with 16 holes to the inch, he decided to use a finer canvas and to work the entire panel himself. Mallard Cottage and Brook Cottage, former homes of the Selbys, are depicted. Sadly, he was not to complete the mammoth task, dying after having finished almost two thirds. Happily, his daughter completed it, incorporating her own 'signature' in the panel – a whippet, in the guise of a cloud formation, to the left of the panel.

Abbotts Ann is an attractive village three miles south west of Andover. Previously 'Anna', it acquired its present name at the beginning of the tenth century when King Edward granted 15 hides of land there to the New Minster at Winchester, later to become Hyde Abbey. And 'little Anna', with five hides, was granted to the Abbey at Wherwell. Earlier, the Romans had settled there, and the remains of a villa of about AD 300 were discovered in 1854. Part of its mosaic floor is now in the British Museum.

Top border

A row of cottages at Little Ann: The cottage on the right with four dormer windows, is Mallard Cottage; *the Old Rectory*: a splendid Georgian house, now a private residence; *three Virgins' Crowns in St Mary's Church*: These represent Abbotts Ann's famous tradition of awarding a crown to any unmarried person, male or female, of unblemished character who was born, baptised and died within the parish. The crown of freshly cut hazelwood, is decorated with black and white paper rosettes. Five paper gauntlets hang from it, challenging anyone who might seek to dispute the award.

The crown is carried high in the funeral cortege by two girls dressed in white and suspended in church for three weeks. If no challenge is made it is hoisted high in the nave with a shield bearing the name and dates of the deceased. Forty-nine crowns survive, the last being awarded in 1973; *the Eagle Inn*: The present building replaced one burned down in 1865 in 'a tremendous conflagration' which destroyed many properties; *a row of cottages* in the centre of the village. The *house with the white palings* is the old School House, behind which is the school. This was built in 1831 by Robert Tasker who arrived as a blacksmith in 1806 and founded the Waterloo Ironworks.

Robert, a nonconformist, stipulated that the school should be open to children of all denominations. The school was leased by the newly-arrived Rector, the Rev. Samuel Best, who became the moving force behind its development. Fees varied with the ability of the parents to pay. More information on Taskers is given in the Upper Clatford panel description.

Middle section

The design for the middle section is a panoramic representation of the old houses of Abbotts and Little Ann from the north. The *white cottage near the T junction* (of Mill Lane with Cattle Lane) in the centre foreground is Brook Cottage. *Two buildings in Mill Lane* are of special interest, Lower Mill (featured in the Domesday Survey of 1086) and the Old Rectory. The mill, too, is now a private residence.

Opposite the Old Rectory is *St Mary's Church*. This was built in 1716 on the site of the former Saxon church by Thomas 'Diamond' Pitt, former Governor of Madras who had acquired the Manor of Abbotts Ann on his return from India in 1710. Whilst there he had bought a huge diamond of 410 carats which he sold at a vast profit to the Regent of France. The church, built in a plain style of red brick, was financed from the proceeds. In the adjacent water meadows are *six lime trees*, survivors of 12 marked on a tithe map of 1730.

The bright red building to the right of the lime trees is the *War Memorial Hall*. The first hall was a hut opened in 1920 which burned down a few years later to be replaced by a brick building which was extended in 1977 to commemorate the Queen's Silver Jubilee.

On the extreme left of the panel, by the side of the old Andover-Salisbury road, is the former *Poplar Farm*, now a restaurant. The main village road, Duck Street, is on the right with the fork to Dunkirt Lane leading into the fields. Before the Enclosure Act of 1774 the fields were sub-divided into strips cultivated by the villagers. 'Dunkirt' probably owes its origin to the nightly run of the dung cart with manure for the strips.

Lower border

This depicts the *Pillhill Brook*, formerly known as the River Anna, and some of the wild life to be seen in the water meadows. They include *woodpeckers*, *hares*, an *exotic hoopoe* and a *heron*. (There is a large heronry in the trees bordering the river in Little Ann.) A *pair of swans* nest along this stretch of water most years and *Canada geese* usually appear during the winter. In addition to various flowers, there is also a *pheasant*, a splendid *barn owl* and a *frog* squatting by the brook.

Little Ann

The Virgins' Crowns at Abbotts Ann

Upper Clatford
Goodworth Clatford
Barton Stacey
Bullington

UPPER CLATFORD, GOODWORTH CLATFORD, BARTON STACEY and BULLINGTON

© Crown copyright licence no. LA079715

The two Clatfords, Upper and Goodworth, are twin villages straddling the River Anton; although they share the same name (Clatford means 'the ford where the burdock grows'), the same school and same Rector, they are in most other respects quite different in character.

UPPER CLATFORD

Top border

Burdock leaves and flowers, symbolising the origin of the name 'Clatford'.

Middle section

In the top centre is *Bury Hill*, a 300 feet high hillfort to the west of the parish, little more than a mile from the centre of Andover. We know that some of Clatford's earliest inhabitants lived here because fragments of haematite-coated pottery found during the 1930s have been dated 6th century BC. The hill is surmounted by three lines of banks and ditches, the outer and the earliest more than half a mile long and dug to a depth of 11 feet 6 inches. The inner ditch was originally 17 feet deep while part of the excavated soil made an inner rampart 7 feet high. The construction of such a defence was a prodigious task suggesting either a powerful local leader able to command the necessary labour force or communities along the Pillhill and Anton united to create a district stronghold. The hillfort appears to have been abandoned about AD 70. Although not another 'Danebury', Bury Hill is of considerable archaeological interest.

The River Test at Upper Clatford

In the top left corner is the parish church of *All Saints*. There was a pre-Conquest church in 'Cladford' but the oldest parts of the present church probably belong to an aisleless 12th century church. In the north window of the belfry are two portions of an inscribed stone, 'Repaired in the Year of the Lord 1578'. The second north aisle and the enlargement of the chancel date from the 1890s and the vestry from 1903.

Part of the Clatfords' history is the firm of Taskers which, for more than 160 years, provided the livelihood for generations of local people. Part of the *Taskers' works* and one of their *traction engines* are depicted on the right. It all began in 1803 when Robert Tasker, a 21 year old blacksmith from near Devizes, worked in the Abbotts Ann forge. A man of vision and enterprise, Robert designed and constructed a plough which proved to be very successful. His brother joined him in 1813 and they found premises in Upper Clatford for their foundry where they made ploughs, other agricultural machinery, cast-iron pumps and domestic appliances. The business prospered and was named the Waterloo Ironworks soon after the Battle in 1815. They built workers' cottages in what became known as Waterloo Square. Their first traction engine, built in

1869, was the first steam engine to be seen on local roads.

By the end of the century various Tasker companies were making engines, threshing tackle, iron bridges and many other products. During World War I the firm made munitions and in World War II huge 'Queen Mary' low-loading trailers capable of carrying a complete fighter aircraft. Large articulated lorry trailers were manufactured here until the early 1980s. Nothing now remains of the ironworks and the site is now a housing estate. The engine in the panel is 'Little Giant', built in 1902.

The bridge with the graceful ornamental arches (lower left) is a fine example of a Tasker iron bridge which crosses the River Anton near the picturesque Fishing Cottage. In the middle centre are the *chalk pits* excavated by the Tasker brothers to provide ballast for the foundations for the works they built on Clatford Marsh. The *arched building* (bottom right corner) was a school built by the Taskers in Anna Valley in 1831. The left-hand side was home for the schoolmistress and her husband and the schoolroom was over the arch to the other side. Now known as The Lodge, it is one of the many listed buildings in the parish.

When the Lodge School was too small, the firm built another school behind the Workmen's Hall.

Lower border

King cups, clumps of which grow in Watery Lane.

Upper Clatford

Goodworth Clatford water tower

The river at Goodworth Clatford

GOODWORTH CLATFORD

Goodworth, the smaller of the two Clatfords, has also been known by the names of 'Lower' and 'Nether'. The Anglo-Saxon derivation of Goodworth is believed to be 'Goda's enclosure', but little is known of Goda.

Top border

A '*nodding donkey*', representing the oil extraction undertaken in the parish for about two years from 1986; a *horse and rider* – there is a riding stable in the village; the *keys of St Peter* on the church crest; *crossed tennis racquets* to represent the flourishing club in the village; a *tractor*, representing farming activities.

Middle section

The *silo* in the upper right corner, a dominant local feature, which commands stunning views over the valley, was built in 1936 as a water tower and was encased in wood. To its left is the *parish church of St Peter* which, until the Dissolution of the monasteries, was a dependency of Wherwell Priory. The church began as a small nave and chancel to which a south aisle was added towards the end of the 12th century.

The 14th century saw the addition of the north aisle and the rebuilding of the tower. Both aisles were rebuilt in the 15th century. A special feature of village life in Goodworth Clatford is the sound of the eight bells in the tower (the oldest cast in 1622), which are regularly rung.

The fine *tree in the fork of the rivers*, where the Pillhill Brook joins the Anton, is a swamp cypress (Taxodium), a native of South America. On the opposite bank are several *pollarded willows*. The *swans* on the river represent the many who are permanent residents; *ducks* can also be seen lower down.

Moseley Cottage (on the right) in the centre of the village, is typical of many thatched properties. Note the *fisherman* on the bank below. The red brick building is the *Village Club*, the hub of village activities and a gift to the village from Sir Alfred Yarrow in 1923. Sir Alfred had built village clubs for two previous parishes where he had lived. He was a generous and enterprising man – and perhaps a little eccentric; he always slept in a rocking hammock as he could not settle in a fixed bed while his own burglar alarm was a device which switched all the lights on in the house simultaneously in the event of an intrusion.

The *crown and the oak tree* symbolise the Royal Oak public house. This, together with the school and Forge Cottages, was destroyed by a flying bomb on the 14th July 1944. There were deaths – refugees from London who had come to Clatford to escape the blitz! The Royal Oak, formerly on a corner site, was later rebuilt about 30 yards away.

Lower border

Burdock; a *heron*; *king cups*; *wild sorrel*; *roe deer*; *willowherb*.

BARTON STACEY AND BULLINGTON

Barton Stacey's earliest inhabitants were the Neolithic tribe who buried their dead in the long barrows, dating from 3500 to 2000 BC, on Moody Down, now the army firing range. There is evidence of a Roman camp east of Manor Farm. In Saxon times the village was Bertun ('ber' or barley and 'tun' or place), a Royal Manor of Edward the Confessor. In 1206 the Manor was bestowed on Sir Rogo de Stacey, hence the name. Barton's sister parish of Bullington lies under the shadow of Tidbury Hill with the ancient hill fort of Tidbury Ring.

Top border

The *blazing house* recalls the great fire which destroyed much of the village on 7th May 1792. A spark from the blacksmith's shop set light to some 'dry litter near a cucumber bed' which in turn ignited the thatch on the adjoining mill house. A strong wind was blowing and soon most of the houses, barns, stables, granaries and ricks were ablaze. One life was lost, that of Farmer Friend who went upstairs to rescue his fortune of 400 guineas. A contemporary report says that only a small piece of his backbone was found

© Crown copyright licence no. LA079715

in the ashes. The fire accounts for the absence of thatched roofs in the village; the *Roman soldier* and his counterpart, the *modern soldier* in combat uniform, symbolise the fact that Army camps have been in the area from Roman to modern times. The large military camp with its many married quarters about a mile from the village centre was built just before World War II. The Allied war time leaders, Sir Winston Churchill and General Dwight Eisenhower, both visited Barton Stacey Camp in 1942 when American troops were stationed there. The camp is now a training unit for the staging of military exercises; the *corn* represents the ancient rights of villagers to thresh corn in the market place.

Swans on the Test

Middle section

The fields at the top of the panel represent those on either side of the road which climbs to Newton Stacey which is separated from Barton Stacey by a stretch of Roman road. The *red flag* flies when the Army firing range at Moody Down is in use, and *hot air balloons* and *helicopters* are a common sight. Below the cornfield a *tractor* is seen at work.

The parish church of *All Saints, Barton Stacey* is in the centre at the foot of the hill. The original church was certainly standing in the 10th century when it was known as St Victor's. During the 12th century it was rebuilt, in the Norman Transitional style. Until the run-down of Barton Stacey Camp it was the official garrison church.

Prominent in the centre is *The Swan Inn*, which is at least 200 years old. Next to it is the *village stores*, *post office* with its *red letter box*, and, most unusually for a village, a launderette. The building whose gables can be seen behind the shop is '*Homelea*', and the *group of houses* above the inn sign represent the view down the village street looking south, including 'Chestnut cottage', home of Mrs J Sambell who designed the panel. The *horse* which can just be seen at centre right is Chammy, owned by Kim and Claire Wainwright.

In the bottom left corner is the *viaduct* which carried the now disused railway over the River Dever and close to it is the picturesque church of *St Michael and All Angels*, Bullington which dates from the 11th century and was built by the Lord of the Manor for the private use of his family and workers. There are *lime trees* lining the church path, representing the twelve apostles. In spring the borders are carpeted with daffodils. Above the church *a man* can be seen *fishing* in the Dever Springs Trout Fisheries, a commercial fishing lake.

Lower border

Deer grazing in Harewood Forest; *poppies*, *hedgehogs*, and *sheep* graze in large numbers; trout are plentiful in the Dever and anglers can hire a rod in the trout fishery; there are many *pheasants* and the area is a habitat for *barn owls*.

Bullington church

*Norman doorway,
Bullington church*

**Chilbolton
Wherwell
Longparish**

CHILBOLTON, WHERWELL and LONGPARISH

© Crown copyright licence no. LA079715

CHILBOLTON

Chilbolton is one of the largest villages in the valley of the River Test just north of its confluence with the Anton. A village of great charm, Chilbolton is a combination of picturesque thatched cottages, modern scientific developments on the old airfield site, and its common, an area with an international botanic reputation. The Test, separating it from Wherwell, forms the northern and western boundaries. Its name at the time of Domesday was Cilbodentune.

Top border

Tracery to be found on Chilbolton's pre-Reformation wafering tongs. Wafers for mid-Lent church ceremonies were baked in Chilbolton before the Normans came. The wafering tongs were used for making these unique wafers for at least three centuries. The tongs belonged to the Baverstock family who passed them, with the secret recipe, from one generation to another. The tongs, made very hot in a wood fire, produced delicately crisp and fragile wafers with ecclesiastical designs, on one side, IS for Jesus the Saviour. They were made

until the 1950s and the tongs are now in Winchester Museum; *King Athelstan* who, tradition says, sought refuge in Chilbolton when harassed by the Danes around 925. It was decided to settle the ensuing seige by combat between their respective champions, Colbrand, the Danish giant, and Guy, Earl of Warwick, in a meadow outside Winchester still called Danesmead. Earl Guy was helped by a friendly crow which fluttered around the Dane, hastening his defeat. The King gave the village to the Cathedral clergy of Holy Trinity, Winchester; *'The Golden Talon'*, emblem of the 17th Airborne Division, U.S. Army. This commemorates the stay from 1944, of the division, with their troop-carrying gliders, on the airfield, living in 'Tent City'. In December of that year the gliders, packed with paratroopers, took part in the 'Battle of the Bulge' in the Belgian Ardennes. Veterans still return and in 1984 a large contingent came over for the 40th anniversary of D-Day presenting Chilbolton with an American flag which had flown on the Capitol in Washington; the *radio telescope* on West Down which can be seen for miles around. The huge dish, 80 ft across, was erected on the old airfield site in 1967 and is a steerable radio aerial operated by the Science Research Council.

Chilbolton

Middle section

A *Spitfire* flies at the top. Chilbolton Down became an airfield, a satellite of Wallop Aerodrome, at the outbreak of World War II. Spitfires flew from here throughout the war and in 1945 thousands of Allied prisoners of war were flown into Chilbolton before their dispersal. Later, the airfield was used by the RAF for testing new jet aircraft, including the Swift and the Vampire. Most of the area was later restored to its former owners. *Fullerton Clump*, a local landmark, is depicted on the left while below is *Chilbolton Common*, declared a Site of Special Scientific Interest. It can be reached by footpath from the village or over the Test from Wherwell. It has never been ploughed or treated with chemicals and is grazed by cattle. Its banks and ditches produce both chalk tolerant and chalk hating plants, well over 100 being recorded by naturalists and scientists. It is also an important nesting site for snipe, redshank and other birds. *Purlygig Bridge* crosses a tributary of the Test. The name is thought to derive from a whirlpool (or whirlygig) under the willows on the Wherwell side of the bridge. *The village grindstone* was presented to the village by Mr Thomas Waterman, publican of the New Inn on the common, to mark the Coronation of King George V and Queen Mary. Mr Waterman was also carpenter, builder, wheelwright, undertaker and steeplejack. For years the grindstone stood under the elm tree outside the village hall and was regularly used by farmhands for sharpening scythes and sickles, but it now stands on the village green, opposite the Abbot's Mitre Inn.

Willow Cottage and *Tudor Cottage*, prominent in the panel, are typical of the attractive houses in the Conservation Area of the village. The *parish church* with the unusual dedication of St Mary-the-Less is seen behind the houses. The chancel is 13th century and the aisles 14th, and an inscription over the vestry door records that the church was restored in 1893. The south west tower and spire, constructed of stone and wood, dates from that restoration. A Lawson's Cypress, planted in the churchyard in 1897 to mark Queen Victoria's Diamond Jubilee, still stands.

Lower border

Death's Head Hawk-Moth (Acherontia atropos) seen in the village; *cowslip* (Primula veris) grows on Chilbolton Common; *lapwing* (Vanellus vanellus) nests on Chilbolton Common.

The Chilbolton Down radio aerial

WHERWELL

Wherwell on the banks of the Test, with many thatched, timbered cottages fronting the winding road, is claimed by many to be one of the most attractive in the Test Valley; it is certainly an amateur photographer's delight. The name, 'Hwerwyl' in AD 955, could have meant 'kettle' or 'cauldron springs' because of its bubbling springs. Pronunciation of the name has always been a problem with variations ranging from 'Wher-well' through 'Wer-rel' to 'Hurrell'.

Wherwell

Bluebells in Harewood Forest

Top border

Euphemia, Abbess of Wherwell Abbey 1226-1257. She seems to have been a medieval Florence Nightingale who, although reputed to be sweet and pious, 'seemed to have the spirit of a man rather than a woman'. She did much to improve the Abbey properties. 'She also, with maternal piety and careful forethought built, for the use of both sick and sound, a new and large farmery away from the main buildings . . . Beneath the farmery she constructed a watercourse, through which a stream flowed with sufficient force to carry off all refuse that might corrupt the air . . .'; a *cockatrice monster*. Legend says that many years ago in a dungeon beneath the priory a duck's egg was hatched by a toad, producing a cockatrice. When small, it was fed and cared for. But it developed into a fearsome monster whose hunger could only be assuaged by a human being. Four acres of land was offered to anyone who could slay the monster and several people lost their lives. Then, a servant named Green had a brilliant idea. He lowered a huge steel mirror into the vault and the cockatrice, seeing another of his kind, battered himself against the mirror for several days. When he was nearly dead the intrepid Green went down and slew him with a spear. In Harewood Forest there is still a four-acre parcel of land known as Green's Acres. A weather-vane depicting the cockatrice was formerly on the church spire but is now in Andover Museum; *Wherwell Abbey*, founded by Queen Elfrida in AD 986. Queen Matilda (Maud) 1102-1167 and King Stephen 1097-1154. *Matilda is seen fleeing from Stephen*, symbolic of the battle between their forces at Wherwell during the 15 year civil war over the succession to the throne. King Henry I made Matilda his heir. But when he died in Normandy in 1135 his nephew, Stephen de Blois, crossed to England and was crowned King in London. Matilda came to England in 1139 and joined forces with her half-brother Robert of Gloucester to contest the succession. In February 1141 Matilda's army defeated Stephen's at the Battle of Lincoln. Stephen was imprisoned in Bristol and on 3rd March, 1141 Matilda was received in state in Winchester Cathedral and elected Domina Anglorum. She proceeded to London, expecting to be crowned, but her arrogance caused a riot and she was forced to flee. Regrouping her forces, she eventually established a garrison in Wherwell Abbey. In September of that year they were defeated in a battle on the outskirts of the village by supporters of Stephen. Many were killed and others took

refuge in the abbey church which was then burned to the ground.

Intermittent fighting between Matilda and Stephen continued for several more years.

Middle section

The houses on the left of the road represent the part of the village believed to be the oldest. Some houses have wattle and daub walls. Above is the *parish church of St Peter and Holy Cross*, reached by a small bridge over the river. The church was restored in 1856-58 and fragments of the old church can be seen here and there in the village.

Above the church is the *White Lion Inn* on the hairpin bend on the road to Andover. The Priory was under siege in the Civil War but the aim of Cromwell's artillery was a little wide and two of his cannon balls are said to have dropped down the chimney of the ivy-covered 17th century inn, half a mile away. One is still on display. On the opposite side of the panel is the *old forge* which, sadly, has fallen into some decay.

Below the forge is *Wherwell Priory*, previously the home of the late Marjorie, Countess of Brecknock. The house is on

Thatched cottages at Wherwell

Church Street, Wherwell

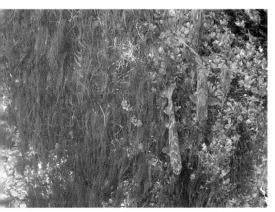

Trout in the Test

the site of the nunnery founded by Queen Elfrida. The story is that King Edgar sent one of his courtiers, Aethelwold, to visit Elfrida, and offer marriage to the King if he considered her beauty equal to the reports. Aethelwold saw that it was and, without revealing the true object of his mission, married her himself, naively reporting that she was a girl of vulgar and commonplace appearance. Inevitably Edgar became aware of his perfidy, and invited himself to Aethelwold's manor in Harewood. The next day, while out hunting in the forest, Edgar murdered him by stabbing him in the back with a javelin. Edgar eventually married Elfrida and they had a son, Ethelred. Legend has it that after Edward's death Elfrida contrived to have Edward (the Martyr), his elder son by his former marriage, murdered at Corfe Castle so that her Ethelred (the Unready) could succeed to the throne. William of Malmesbury tells how Elfrida founded the Abbey at Wherwell, possibly as an act of penitence. The nunnery flourished until it was destroyed by Henry VIII in 1540. Nothing now remains of the Abbey but Wherwell Priory, a lovely old mansion, was built near the site.

The War Memorial with the adjacent cherry tree is depicted in the centre of the panel. The tree is no longer there, having been a casualty of the great 1987 gale. *The Test* flows beneath the bridge at the end of the road.

Lower border

Sheep; *mallard*, *swan* and *cygnet* on the Test; *pheasant*; *fallow deer* in Harewood Forest.

LONGPARISH

Longparish is a most apt name for the village as it is, indeed, a long parish, winding and twisting for three miles along the Test. The name did not appear until the middle of the 16th century, at about the time of the Dissolution of the Monasteries, before which it was known as Middleton (or Middletune).

The parish was formed from four ancient 'tithings', East and West Aston, Middleton and Forton. Apart from some postwar development of council housing, Longparish remains much as it has for centuries, with half-timbered, brick and flint cottages.

Top border

The first item refers to the *murder of Aethelwold* by King Edgar, recounted in the description of the Wherwell panel. A monument in Harewood Forest, erected in 1825 by Lt Col William Iremonger and known as Deadman's Plack, is inscribed as follows: 'About the Year of our Lord DCCCCLXIII Upon this Spot beyond Time of Memory. Called Deadman's Plack tradition reports that Edgar (Surnamed the

Peaceable) King of England in the ardor of Youth Love and Indignation Slew with his own hand his treacherous and ungrateful Favourite Earl Athelwold owner of this forest of Harewood in resentment of the Earl's having basely betrayed his Royal confidence and perfidiously married his Intended Bride The beauteous Elfrida Daughter of Ordgar Earl of Devonshire, afterwards Wife to King Edward and by him mother of King Etheldred II, which Queen Elfrida after Edgar's death murdered his eldest son King Edward the Martyr and founded "The Nunnery of Wherwell"'; *Ashburn Rest* – an oak seat at a spring where, at one time, a drinking cup was fastened to the stone rim. It was erected by the Revd Burnaby-Green in 1886 for rest and refreshment of his parishioners, on their long walk to church. On it is carved, 'O ye wells, Bless ye the Lord, Praise Him and magnify him for ever'; the *stocks* are outside the churchyard wall near the east lychgate. In 1936, due to an unfortunate misunder-standing of instructions, they were replaced by stout new ones! There is no record of when they were last used; *Father Time*, the famous weather vane on the roof of Lords cricket ground, recalls the notable achievement of the Longparish Cricket Club in winning the Samuel Whitbread

Deadman's Plack monument

85

View towards Longparish Church

competition at Lords on 31st August 1987. Cricket at Longparish has a long history with records going back to 1878. In 1987 they played Treeton Welfare from Yorkshire, beating them by 76 runs and taking the cup home in triumph.

Middle section

The *houses* just below the skyline at the top are those at Forton at the west end of the village. The *church of St Nicholas* on the left was built between 1100 and 1200 but the chief features remaining of the original building are the nave arcades. As a memorial of the Silver Jubilee of King George V, the village subscribed to the re-hanging of the bells with one new bell to make a peal of six. In 1950 Longparish celebrated the 750th anniversary of the building of the church.

Further down the road is *the school*. This was opened in 1837 by the 'National Society for promoting the education of the poor in the principles of the Established Church'. In 1957 a new Church of England (Aided) School was built, which caters for children of primary school age from Longparish and Hurstbourne Priors with about 70 pupils. The Test flows past the boundary fence of the school site.

Opposite the church is the *village hall*, whose site was conveyed to the Diocesan Board of Finance in 1910 for the building of a church hall. In 1963 a new charity was established which leased the Longparish Village Hall to the Parish Council for a peppercorn rent, its administration being in the hands of a village management committee.

The charming *thatched cottage* below the village hall is the Old Curacy, typical of many such in the village, and below that, *The Plough public house*, one of the village's two inns. It was built during the 19th century and backs on to the Test.

Opposite is the house of *The Upper Mill* with the bridge crossing diagonally in front. This is one of two mills in the village (both mentioned in the Domesday Survey) and it is currently being restored by its owner, who has recovered three or four millstones from the river, refurbished some of the machinery and replaced some of the timber on the water wheel.

The River Test, bridged in many places and bordered by lush meadows, is a prominent feature of the village. The stretch featured in the panel, with the line of weeping willows, bullrushes, fungi and various water meadow plants, together with the bridge and the ducks, is representative of the section of the river in the village.

Lower border

Heron; *roe deer*; *mute swan*; *trout* and *kingfisher*.

Paper Mill Farm, Longparish

The river at Longparish

The Wallops
(Nether Wallop and Over Wallop)

THE WALLOPS

THE WALLOPS (NETHER WALLOP and OVER WALLOP)

© Crown copyright licence no. LA079715

Strung along three miles of the Wallop Brook on its way to join the Test at Bossington are the three villages which take their name from the chalk stream – Nether, Middle and Over Wallop. The name derives from 'waella' (street) and 'hop' (valley) or, put more poetically, the place of springing water. Nether and Over are highly attractive villages; Middle Wallop lies between the two, clustered around the busy crossroads, and is the home of the School of Army Aviation. In The Wallops panel, Nether is on the left and Over on the right.

NETHER WALLOP

Nether Wallop follows the course of the stream for about a mile and a half, the church and village being clustered in the main bend.

Top border

Tawny owl; *pheasant*; *kingfisher*; *Paulet Coat of Arms*. It was in 1547 that Sir William Paulet, later first Marquis of Winchester, bought the Chief Manor of Nether Wallop, beginning the overlordship of the Paulet or Powlett family that was to last for 364 years; *nightingale*; *swallow*; *curlew*; *nuthatch*.

Middle section

The *helicopter* (top left) is from The School of Army Aviation based at the former RAF station built between 1938 and 1940. Throughout the war the airfield was a front line fighter station, bombed on several occasions. The Army Air Corps facility now occupies land in both Over and Nether Wallop parishes. Today it is the operational training centre for Army Aviation; its helicopter pilots overfly most villages in the district. The *airfield building* and the *red wind sock* can be seen on the left. The airfield is also the home of the Museum of

Army Air Corps Lynx over Middle Wallop Airfield

Army Flying. The School of Army Aviation, previously the Army Air Corps Centre, has the Freedom of the Borough of Test Valley 'with the right, honour and distinction of marching through the streets of the Borough on all ceremonial occasions with colours flying, bands playing, drums beating and bayonets fixed'.

At the top is *Danebury Hill Fort*, one of the finest Iron Age camps in Hampshire. Danebury Ring has acquired international archaeological importance as a result of the excavations carried out under the direction of Professor Barry Cunliffe. The largest excavation on a prehistoric site in Britain has revealed an unparalleled view of life in an Iron Age Hill Fort from about 600 BC to 50 AD. *Farming activities* are illustrated below Danebury and *two riders* are also to be seen. The building in the top right corner is *Fifehead Manor*, which legend links with Lady Godiva.

In the centre is the *parish church of St Andrew*. The original church was built about 50 years before the Norman Conquest when Nether Wallop belonged to Earl Godwin. The Normans enlarged it and built a west tower. Later, a steeple was added which lasted until 1704 when, it is recorded, 'The Tower of Wallop Church fell down, the walls being quite rotten and decayed'. In the nave is the only known brass to an Abbess, Mary Gore, who died in 1436 and was buried in the church.

To the right of the church is the unusual 15 ft high *pyramid memorial* to Dr Francis Douce who died in 1760. He left money in his will 'that boys and girls in the parish are taught to read and write and cast an account a little way, but they must not go too far least it makes them saucy and the girls all want to be chamber maids, and in a few years you will be in want of cooks'.

The large house to the left of the church is *Garlogs* (thought to be a corruption of Gore's Lodge), the home of the aforementioned Abbess. The fact that she was buried in the church suggests that she may well have been a local girl made good. A tunnel is said to have linked the house with 'Monks' in the centre of the village. A later occupier was the brilliant jockey and trainer, Tom Cannon, great-grandfather of Lester Piggott. He developed Danebury into one of the finest stables in the country. The house with the large chimney stacks to the right of the church is the former *Wallop House*, built in 1838 on the site of the nunnery and now

View towards Danebury, with the Grandstand

Detail of mural in Nether Wallop church

91

St Andrew's church and Nether Wallop

Winton House Nursing Home.

In the centre foreground is *the Mill* which was in full use until 1949 not only as a mill but also as a bakery. Now it houses a fishing tackle and trout-breeding business. At the rear of the *group of cottages* on the right is the *village hall*. Running across the whole panel is the *Wallop Brook* with *willow trees* on the bank. Some of the first cricket bats were made from Wallop willows, including those used by the great Dr W G Grace. In the bottom left corner is *Place Farm* on a site probably occupied before the Conquest. Later it was the home of the Paulets, and more recently, of the celebrated conductor Leopold Stokowski.

Lower border

Flora found in the locality, including *wild arum*, *bluebells*, *dandelion clocks* and *foxglove*. Amongst the flowers is a *rabbit* and a *snail*.

OVER WALLOP

Over Wallop was described in the Domesday Book as the 'other Wallop', smaller than Nether. At the time of the Conquest it was held by King Harold, having been the home of his mother, Countess Gueda. It is here, in Townsend Field, that the Wallop Brook rises. From earliest times the main street has followed the north side of the brook, properties on the other side using plank bridges to cross.

Top border

Green woodpecker; *cuckoo*; *magpie*; *Wallop Coat of Arms*, with its heraldic 'river'. In 1208 Matthew Wallop, Warden of Winchester, was granted land in the village. One of the panels of the 15th century font bears the crest of the family. One branch became Earls of Portsmouth who owned the greater part of Over Wallop for four centuries; *green plover*; *barn owl*.

Middle section

The background at the top represents farming activities, with *grazing sheep*, a *tractor* ploughing and a *cornfield*.

The house in the top left corner is *Blacksmiths Farm*. This was built in the early 18th century of brick and flint, an annexe being added in 1852. The timber-framed and thatched cottage in the centre is *South View*, with wattle and daub walls dating from about 1540. The small rectangle in the roof is reputed to be the smugglers' window, from which the excise men could be seen approaching. Next to it is the *White Hart Inn*, an early 18th century coaching inn. Beer was brewed there and evidence of the vats can be seen in the cellars.

On 16 February 1982 the roof was destroyed by fire. During the conflagration one or two regulars were loath to leave the bar!

On the left in the next row is *Forresters*, an elegant Queen Anne house, the home for several generations of the Clarke family who were local builders. The two buildings on the other side of the War memorial are the *Church Farm barn and house*, home to generations of the Shadwell family. The 18th century barn has both chalk cob and boarded walls and a thatched roof. It is still in use. In front can be seen three of the family's herd of *Guernsey cows* which twice a day make their slow 200 yard trek between grazing and milking. Until 1992 the family ran its own milk round. Some wheat grown on the farm's 100 acres is for thatching.

The *War Memorial Cross* in the centre of the panel, listing the 19 from the village who had fallen in the war, was unveiled in October 1919. Glider Pilot Regiment veterans regularly attend Remembrance Day services. In the bottom left corner is *King's Farm*. This attractive early Georgian house at the foot of Orange Lane is brick built, partly timber framed and bears the date 1738. Orange Lane is so called because tradition has it that Wallop had the honour of accommodating William of Orange and his army en route from Brixham to London but recent research indicates that his progress was well to the west of the village. It could well, however, have had repercussions in the village.

In the centre at the bottom is *St Peter's Church Hall*. Built in 1853 (for £255) it served as the Church School until 1895 when the Council School was opened.

St Peter's Church occupies the bottom right corner. It underwent a major restoration in 1866 under the supervision of J L Pearson, architect to Truro Cathedral, but the 15th century octagonal font and the 13th century piscina were retained. The 'saddleback' bell tower houses five bells, the oldest dated 1631.

Lower border

This continues the Nether Wallop theme of *wild flowers* found locally, with a hovering *damsel fly*.

The Wallop Brook

Stockbridge
Longstock
Leckford

The BOROUGH of TEST VALLEY

DEG·TESTE·VALEMIT

Linkenholt
Vernham Faccombe
Dean
Hurstbourne Tarrant

Tangley
Fyfield   Smannell
Appleshaw Charlton
Kimpton Penton Grafton
Thruxton Andover
South Tedworth ynll   Penton Mewsey
Amport   Longparish
Shipton Bellinger Monxton Upper Clatford
Quarley Abbotts Ann Goodworth Clatford
Grateley   Bullington
Wherwell Barton Stacey
Over Wallop Longstock Chilbolton
Nether Wallop   Leckford
Stockbridge
Broughton Houghton Little Somborne
Buckholt
Bossington
West Tytherley   Ashley
Kings Somborne
East Tytherley
Frenchmoor
East Dean Mottisfont Braishfield
Lockerly Michelmarsh
Sherfield English Awbridge Ampfield
Melchet Park Romsey
Plaitford   North Baddesley
Wellow
Chilworth
Nursling
Rownhams

I chatter, chatter, as I flow
to join the brimming river;
For men may come and men may go,
But I go on for ever.

From Tennyson's The Brook
quoted by Lord Denning at
the first public exhibition
June 1990

Robina Orchard

STOCKBRIDGE
LONGSTOCK
LECKFORD

STOCKBRIDGE, LONGSTOCK and LECKFORD

© Crown copyright licence no. LA079715

The decision to include a map of the Borough was taken during discussions on what should fill the space next to the Stockbridge, Longstock and Leckford section.

The verse, from 'The Brook' by Alfred, Lord Tennyson, was quoted by Lord Denning at the first public showing of the panels in Andover Museum in July 1990.

STOCKBRIDGE

On a causeway of compressed chalk laid down in the remote past for a crossing of the River Test, Stockbridge is almost midway between Andover to the north and Romsey to the south. There have been settlements on Stockbridge Down since at least the second millennium BC; within a short distance are the impressive earthworks at Danebury, Meon Hill and Woolbury. Two ancient roads meet and cross at Stockbridge, one running east to west between Winchester and Old Sarum, later Salisbury, and the other running north and south along the valley of the Test. The prosperity of Stockbridge has always stemmed largely from the roads which pass through it.

The 'town' (actually little more than a single row of buildings on each side of the wide main street) grew in importance when Welsh drovers rested there with their flocks on their way to various sheep fairs and markets. A thatched cottage known as 'Drovers House' has the message in Welsh painted on the wall: 'Seasoned hay, tasty pastures, good beer, comfortable beds'.

Top border

A peat spade. For centuries peat was dug in the valley, notably at Longstock and Stockbridge. Tradition has it that farmers would grant their labourers an annual day off work to cut peat and allow them the use of a farm cart to carry it home; a *Danish ship*: this is a reminder of the days when the Test was navigable and Danish invaders are thought to have dug a wide channel in the water meadows at Longstock for their flat bottomed boats. The channel was about 300 feet long and the excavated earth was piled up to form a primitive quay. The 'dock' probably served both as a base for further exploration and for the despatch of looted goods; *an eel trap, fishing flies, trout and net*: the Test, 'the queen of chalk streams', has served the angler well. Many claim it to be the finest trout stream in the world. The artificial flies are typical of the very realistic and intriguingly named creations tied so lovingly by enthusiasts.

The Stockbridge Silver Mace is part of the regalia of ancient Court Leets and Baron: The Courts are a survival of a system of jurisdiction of the Middle Ages for the settlement of local disputes, the maintenance of common pastures and ditches and the punishment of minor offences.

The Lord of the manor presided over the annual courts whose officers were a Bailiff, a Constable (now called Sergeant-at-Mace) and Hayward. From 1563 to 1832 Stockbridge was a Borough with the right to return two Members to Parliament. The Bailiff organised the voting system which was subject to considerable corruption. The Mace and Seal both having been given to the Borough as bribes, are evidence of such corruption. The Mace came from an aspiring candidate, Essex Strode, in 1681 and bore the arms of the sovereign and the donor together with an inscription (in Latin): 'Here I am, a glory to Stockbridge, by the gift of Essex Strode.' In spite of his bribe, Strode was defeated by an opponent who paid cash. Stockbridge kept the Mace! The Courts were in abeyance for almost 30 years from 1891 when Hicks Lancashire pawned the manor to recoup losses incurred over a court case which had been taken to the House of Lords by the inhabitants of Stockbridge when he attempted to appropriate the Common Down. Fortunately the mace, seal and Hayward's staff were retained by the steward of the manor who knew that they did not belong to Lancashire.

In 1920 they were handed over to Norman Hill, a Liverpool solicitor who had retired

The main street of Stockbridge

Stokes' Garage

to Stockbridge. In 1921 he reinstated the ceremony of the Courts. After his death in 1944 the manor passed to his daughter, historian Professor Rosalind Hill, and in March 1994 there were great celebrations at Stockbridge to mark the 50th anniversary of her unique service as Quondam Lady of the Manor. The National Trust now holds the Lordship.

Middle section

At the top on the left is the *parish church of St Nicholas, Leckford* and its lychgate. The church, with flint walls and small weather-board bell turret, dates from the 15th century, but the chancel was rebuilt early in the 16th century out of alignment with the nave, probably to allow space for processions between the church and the churchyard boundary. Much of the village is owned by the John Lewis Partnership whose Water Gardens at Longstock are a spectacular feature and are open to the public on one Sunday each month in the summer. Below the church is the *Peat Spade public house* and the *parish church of St Mary, Longstock*, with its lychgate. The church is comparatively modern (1876/1880) but designed in the style of the 13th century. The tower contains five bells.

In front of the church is an example of the *thatched fishing huts* which are an attractive feature of this stretch of the river. On the opposite bank is an *angler* who seems to have made a catch.

To the top right is the *chancel of the old chapel of St Peter*, dating from the 12th century. All but the nave was demolished in 1866 and it gradually fell into disrepair. In 1963, however, it was re-hallowed and since then has been extensively refurbished. Below is the *parish church of St Peter*, built in the 1860s.

To the left of old St Peter's Church is the distinctive *Town Hall*, built about 1810 at his own expense by John Foster Barham who represented the Borough for many years in Parliament. By 1820 he owned at least 80 houses in Stockbridge, but following a financial setback in 1822, sold 72 of his houses to his political opponent, Lord Grosvenor, and applied for the Chiltern Hundreds. Note the *two red telephone kiosks* near the Town Hall. When the panel was worked their days were thought to be numbered but they are still there!

Lord Grosvenor's name is perpetuated by the *Grosvenor Hotel*, an attractive building with the large porch and upper room supported on slender columns. The old market hall is incorporated into the hotel. The room above the porch is the private sanctum of the Houghton Fishing Club, the most prestigious club for dry-fly fishermen in the country, founded in 1822. The Houghton Club is limited to 17 members and records are kept of every fish taken and the fly used.

Race horses can just be seen on the sky line above the Town Hall. Racing was held for decades on a racecourse below Danebury from where the remains of the grandstand can still be seen. King Edward VII, when Prince of Wales, was a regular visitor, delighting boys by throwing pennies to them from his carriage.

Lower border

The flora and fauna of the Test Valley: *cows*; *dragonflies*; *ducks*; a *trout*; a really splendid *cockerel*.

Eel traps at Longstock

Longstock village

Houghton
Bossington
Broughton

HOUGHTON, BOSSINGTON and BROUGHTON

© Crown copyright licence no. LA079715

Houghton gives its name to the exclusive fishing club whose headquarters are in Stockbridge but whose stretch of the Test flows through the parish. Broughton, with its many timbered and flower-bedecked thatched cottages, two miles away on the Wallop Brook, is one of the largest villages in Test Valley. In between is Bossington House whose owner in 1829 destroyed the surrounding hamlet.

HOUGHTON AND BOSSINGTON

Top border

A *game keeper and his dog*, representing local shooting interests; a *barge* loaded with locally cut chalk blocks which would have been transported along the Redbridge to Andover canal (Mendip lead, bearing the name of the Emperor Nero and dated AD 59, was unearthed at Bossington in 1783 during excavations for the canal); *Henry V's army* under the Earl of Huntingdon camped at Bossington before leaving for France and the Battle of Agincourt in 1415. Henry is said to have attended the church at Bossington and a local field is still called Agincourt; a *wool merchant* loading his mule and a *sheep shearer*. Sheep were driven through Houghton on their way to sheep fairs in Stockbridge and Weyhill; a *soldier*, representing those who served in both world wars; a *Roman centurion*. The Roman road from Winchester to Sarum passed close by.

The river at Houghton Mill

Middle section

Houghton's 12th century *All Saints Church* is in the centre. Unusually, there are 3 arched arcades in the south aisle but only 2 in the north. On some columns can be seen medieval crosses carved by pilgrims on their way to St Swithun's shrine at Winchester. To the left of the church is the *sheepbridge* arching over the river with the poplar trees beyond and part of *Houghton Lodge*, built by the river about 1800 and now noted for its magnificent display of daffodils at Easter. Above the church roof is *Bossington House*, with its cedar tree, home of John Fairey of the aviation family. He flies his *Fairey Flycatcher* over the house. *Hereford cattle* graze below the bridge and nearby a *badger* can be seen. In the left foreground is the *Boot Inn*, and beyond are *Wayside Cottages*, originally built for the Inn's ostlers. To the right is the well-known *wheelright's workshop* in front of which is a *thatcher*, with his straw bundles, about to work on one of the cottages. A *fisherman* wades in the river while a *swan* floats gracefully by the *willow tree*. A *kestrel* hovers and *mallards* are on the wing above *Houghton Lodge*.

Lower border

The *bullrush, yellow mimulus, water avens, moorhen, water rail* and *orange balsam* represent the wildlife of the river and water meadows as do the *trout, grey wagtail, kingfisher, marsh marigold, shrew* and *barn owl*. The *hare, tiger moth, wild strawberry, field bindweed, red squirrel, orange tip butterfly, rosebay willowherb* and *ragged robin* are all to be found in the surrounding countryside.

John Fairey with a replica Fairey Flycatcher

Bossington Church

BROUGHTON

Top border

To the right of the centurion, the shepherd represents the ancient sheep drove which passed through Broughton on its way to the Stockbridge and Weyhill sheep fairs: the *juggler*, the *girl carrying produce*, the *stall*, the *King* and the *goosegirl* all represent the granting by Henry III in 1248 of a weekly market at the Manor of Broughton and a yearly fair on the feast of St Mary Magdalene; the next figures are *William Steele and his daughter Anne*. In 1699 William Steele was ordained Baptist Pastor. Anne wrote 144 hymns, 34 psalms and about 50 poems; *two boys* stand in front of the school endowed in 1601 by Thomas Dowse, Lord of the Manor of Broughton, for a schoolmaster to teach children to read, write and understand arithmetic. The charity is still administered by the Rector and trustees; a *village blacksmith*. Once there were six blacksmiths in Broughton; above him is the *sign of the greyhound*, now used by one of the public houses and originally part of the arms of Thomas Dowse.

Middle section

In the centre is the *dovecote* or columbarium in the graveyard of the church. The present structure was built in 1684 on the site of one built in 1340. There are 482 'L'-shaped nesting boxes in the thickness of the walls. The oldest part of the parish *church of St Mary the Virgin* dates from the 12th century. About 1220 the nave was lengthened and the present west door built, while the tower was added in the fifteenth century. In the churchyard are ancient *Irish yews*. The *church clock* is set at eight o'clock, a reminder that until 1963 a curfew bell was rung daily at 8pm from Michaelmas Day to Lady Day to tell householders to douse their fires to minimise the risk to thatched roofs.

In the centre right of the main section is the *Baptist Chapel* which dates from 1816 with a reminder on the stone on the front of the building that the Baptist faith was established in Broughton in 1655. The pews were made from timbers from HMS 'The Royal George'. The *houses* between the Baptist Church and the Dovecote are modern village homes, whilst that between the dovecote and the parish church represents the many *thatched cottages*. In the background is *Broughton Down*, with the chalk track up to Whiteshoot

Broughton dovecote

Hill on the right. Below this are *fields* of hay, corn and grazing cattle and horses, all part of village farming. Just visible at the top right of the Baptist Church is the village *community bus* which, with volunteer drivers, operates regular services to Romsey, Salisbury, Winchester and Southampton.

The *deer*, *heron*, *wild duck*, *swans* and *willow trees* are all seen on or near the Wallop Brook as it flows through the village to join the Test at Bossington. The two *horseriders* near the bridge and the *pheasants* in the foreground represent sporting pursuits, while the Hampshire Down *sheep* in the corner are another indication of the agricultural nature of Broughton.

Lower border

The *barn owl* in flight (shared with the Houghton section), *mallard*, *flag iris* and *water crowfoot* are all found in the Wallop Brook and adjacent water meadows. The *harebell*, *spotted woodpecker*, *stoat*, *dog rose*, *rabbit*, *lapwing* and *fox* live in the surrounding countryside. The *chalk blue butterfly* feeding on *horseshoe vetch*, the *orchid* and the *cowslip* are denizens of Broughton Down while the *ears of wheat*, the *mayweed* and the *poppy* represent the arable fields.

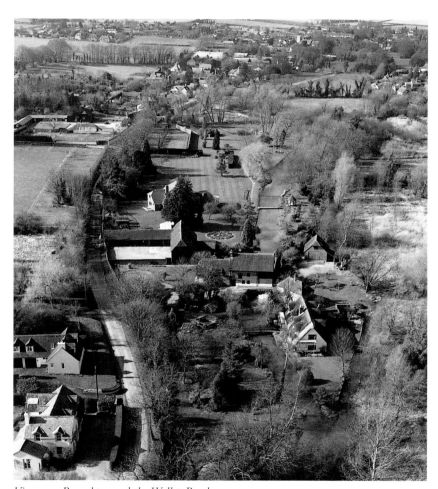

View over Broughton and the Wallop Brook

King's Somborne
Little Somborne
Up Somborne
Ashley

KING'S SOMBORNE, LITTLE SOMBORNE, UP SOMBORNE and ASHLEY

© Crown copyright licence no. LA079715

The 'Sombornes' comprise the scattered village of King's Somborne, with its centre clustered attractively around the parish church and the village green, together with the hamlets of Up Somborne, Ashley and Eldon. Up Somborne, three miles from the village itself, has a cherished gem of a church of Saxon origin now redundant but restored. Ashley, the 'gateway' to Farley Mount has its own redundant church as has lonely Eldon, once the smallest parish in England, with yet a third redundant church in a lawn in front of a farm house. The parish of Somborne with Ashley must surely be the only one in the United Kingdom with three restored, redundant churches.

Flowing through the village is the Somborne stream which rises beyond Up Somborne towards the Rack and Manger public house on the A272 and joins the Test at Horsebridge. Normally a well behaved, short-lived bourne, it flooded extensively in the spring of 1994 and far worse yet again in 1995 causing much distress and the evacuation of several cottages.

Archaeological excavations during the 1980s in the churchyard, Old Palace Farm and on the school site suggests that there was an important Saxon settlement in the area. At the time of Domesday, Somborne was part of the royal demesne.

John of Gaunt, fourth son of King Edward III, inherited the manor through his first wife, Blanche, daughter of the first Duke of Lancaster. Their son, Henry of Bolingbroke, became King Henry IV in 1399. The banks of the John of Gaunt Deer Park can still be traced between the village and the River Test but there is little evidence for the attractive notion that he resided here for any length of time or hunted in his park.

The village achieved renown through the Vicar, the Revd Richard Dawes, later Dean of Hereford, who, in 1842, founded the village school which, owing to his visionary educational philosophy, was widely regarded as a model of its kind.

Top border

A Crusader with shield and banner, the *crest of the Hervey-Bathurst family* of Somborne Park; *a motte and bailey castle* built about 1100 at Ashley, then part of the Royal Forest of Bere; a *Roman centurion*: the Roman road from Winchester to Old Sarum passed through the parish; the *monument at Farley Mount*, actually a few yards outside the Test Valley Borough Boundary, was erected on top of a Bronze Age burial mound as a memorial to a horse, later known as 'Beware Chalk Pit', which survived with its rider after jumping into a 25 feet-deep chalk pit. The next year it went on to win the 1734 Hunters Cup at Worthy Down. The horse is buried under the monument; a German *Junkers 88* bomber was shot down in the village by a Spitfire on 21 September 1940, during the Battle of Britain, the crew of four being killed. In 1951 a memorial stone to them was erected a few yards outside the Test Valley Borough boundary, at Hoplands, incorrectly recording the date as 23 September; *the brasses* (c1380) in the chancel of the church, traditionally thought to be of John of Gaunt's stewards, father and son; the *Revd Richard Dawes*, Vicar 1836-1850 who founded the village school: *John of Gaunt's archery butt*, the protected

mound of which is still in a local garden; representation of *local organisations* including uniformed groups and the WI; the *'Sprat and Winkle' line*: which opened in 1865, running from Southampton to Andover along the line of the old canal. Somborne was served by Horsebridge Station but the line closed in September 1964; *John of Gaunt*, born in 1340 the third son of King Edward III; the *crest of Sir Thomas Sopwith*, the aviation pioneer, who lived at Compton Manor for more than 40 years and died there in 1989 at the age of 101; a World War I *Sopwith Camel* and his *yacht 'Endeavour'* in which he competed for the Americas' Cup.

Little Somborne Church

Middle section

Prominent in the centre of the panel, thanks to the generosity of Herbert Johnson of Marsh Court, is the elegant *War Memorial* designed by Lutyens. Behind it is the *parish church of St Peter and St Paul* largely the result of a major Victorian restoration in 1885 but a section of the south arcades of the nave dates from about 1240. The font is, however, Norman, the only relic of the earlier church.

To the right of the church is the Revd Richard Dawes' *school* of 1842. His ideas were in some ways almost a century ahead of his times both educationally and socially. The school soon acquired national recognition and Dawes was encouraged to write extensively about it, his pamphlets having a great influence on 19th century educational thought and practice.

To the left of the church is the 18th century thatched *Crown Inn* and the adjacent *Crown Cottage* with fine topiary work. Above the War Memorial is the 15th century *Cruck Cottage*, a typical two-bay cruck, the three 'cruck' tresses of naturally bent oak trees forming the framework for two rooms and supporting the roof. Between Cruck Cottage and the tower of the church is a field of *oil-seed rape*, a fairly new farming feature when the panel was worked.

In the bottom left hand corner is *Marsh Court*. This remarkable house was built of chalk by Sir Edwin Lutyens for financier Herbert Johnson, between 1901 and 1904. Gertrude Jeckyll designed the gardens. In 1926 the ballroom, also designed by Lutyens, was added. For more than forty years, until 1989, Marsh Court housed a prep school but in 1993 it was purchased for massive

refurbishment as a family home for an MP. Above Marsh Court is the restored gem of a *Saxon Church* at Little Somborne, and *Somborne Park*, seat of the Hervey-Bathursts. The church was declared redundant in 1974 and was fully restored by the Redundant Churches Fund in 1976-77, when archaeologists recorded in detail every part of the structure. Sir Thomas and Lady Sopwith are buried in the churchyard.

Up Somborne, a small farming village, is in the top left hand corner of the panel. A *combine harvester* is at work in a cornfield and a *tractor* ploughing in another. To the right of Up Somborne is *Ashley* with the little *church of St Mary*. This was also declared redundant in 1976 and subsequently extensively restored. The fine specimen *yew tree* was blown down in the great gale. The thatched *ancient well*, long a picturesque feature, was burned down by vandals in 1991 but restored with a tiled roof by the people of Ashley in 1993. To the right of the church is *Ashley Manor*. The pool in front of the house is one of a series of pools and pens which house the unique Ashley Waterfowl Collection of rare and endangered species. The *thatched cottage* is 'Little Thatches' which also has internal cruck beams. The *memorial on Farley Mount* can just be seen on the skyline. To the right of Ashley is *Hoplands*, an equestrian area, and, below it, the retirement cottages in *Humber View*. The small farming hamlet of *Eldon* is seen in the top right hand corner. The small, redundant chapel is in the farm complex. Eldon is now well-known for its rare breed of pigs and sausage manufacture.

Flying over *Compton Manor*, the former home of the late Sir Thomas Sopwith, is a *red Wessex helicopter* of the Queen's Flight used by Prince Charles who, with other members of the Royal Family, often enjoyed the excellent shooting on the estate. The *chalk pits* at Brook are a local landmark. In the lower right hand corner is *Horsebridge Mill*, one of three mentioned in the Domesday Survey, now used for the manufacture of scientific measuring instruments. Behind the mill is part of *John of Gaunt's deer park*.

Two long distance footpaths, the Test Way along the old railway, and the Clarendon Way from Winchester to Salisbury, cross in the village. The *walkers* in the bottom left hand corner represent the many ramblers who pass through the village. At the other side of the panel the late *Mike Simms* is seen fishing in the John of Gaunt lake which he established. Two *local children* by the stream

watch the swans while Ian Wilson's *bull terrier*, Puckeridge, waits patiently.

Lower border

Increasingly rare *barn owls*; *snowdrop* and *poppy*; *butterflies* including the rare Chalk Blue; *kingfisher* and *heron*; *lilies of the valley*, *pheasants*; the *parish names*, *panel date* and *fruit*; *pedigree cow and bull*; *cowslips*; *foxes*; the rare *green fritillary*; *sheep*, *pig* and *deer*; rare varieties of *orchid*.

Horsebridge Mill

Horsebridge Station

Mottisfont
Nursling and Rownhams
East Tytherley

MOTTISFONT, NURSLING and ROWNHAMS, and EAST TYTHERLEY

© Crown copyright licence no. LA079715

Mottisfont Abbey

MOTTISFONT

Mottisfont would not be of such interest were it not for the magnificent Abbey, built in the water meadows by the River Test, around which the village grew up.

Top border

The *bears and ragged staff* in the centre represent the coat of arms of the Barker-Mills family which acquired the Abbey House in 1684. Stone chained bears are mounted on the gate piers to both entrances; the *tiles on either side* show the 13th century tiles from the floor of the Priory, found in rubble in nearby fields. A number were built into the Abbey summerhouse during the 18th century.

Middle section

At the centre is *Mottisfont Abbey* which is surrounded by magnificent grounds with spacious lawns and mammoth plane, cedar, chestnut and beech trees. In the garden is a crystal clear spring which flows at 200 gallons a minute to join the Test, and an ice house, one of two in the village.

The Priory of Holy Trinity was established in 1201 by William Briwere, an officer of Richard I.

It was suppressed at the Dissolution and in 1536 was given by Henry VIII to Lord Sandys, his Lord Chamberlain, in return for the villages of Chelsea and Paddington! He adapted it for domestic use, siting the main rooms in the nave. The 'new' façade was built for Sir Richard Mill in 1743.

Until 1934 the Abbey remained in the ownership of Lord Sandys' family, albeit with several changes of name. In 1934 it was bought by Gilbert Russell on whose death in 1957 the house passed to the National Trust.

The *parish church of St Andrew* dates in part from the first half of the 12th Century, the chancel being extended three centuries later. It houses a rare 17th century clock movement.

In the top right corner is the *Post Office*, for many years the village stores, which is now renowned for its cream teas. In the top left corner is the *Mill Arms* at Dunbridge, once a coaching inn. The long, low white extension is now a popular skittle alley.

Below the Abbey is a beautiful stretch of the Test and in the foreground the famous *Mottisfont or Oakley Oak* tree which is probably more than a thousand years old. It is now hollow and cows have often calved inside it.

Lower border

The *roses* on either side represent the rose garden laid out in 1972 by Graham Stuart Thomas as a show place for the National Trust's collection of historic roses which he had gathered during his long career as its Garden Adviser. There are now more than 340 named varieties in the collection. In between are some of the fauna and flora which abound in and around the village: the *deer, Canada geese, swans, primroses, Speckled Wood butterfly* and a *barn owl*.

NURSLING and ROWNHAMS

The ancient settlement of Nursling, formerly Nutshalling ('the nut grove by the water meadows') now with a post-war shopping centre, housing estates, hall and school, is divided by the M27 motorway from the Victorian village of Rownhams, also extended by substantial post-war development.

Top border

In the centre is *St. Boniface*, named 'Winfrith' when he was born in Crediton in 680. After studying at the Benedictine Abbey at Exeter he became Abbott of the monastery at Nursling in 717. Two years later as Boniface he was given a Papal commission to conduct an evangelical mission to what is now Germany. In 754 he and fifty of his followers were murdered by a heathen mob; the *two crests* are those of the *Barker-Mills family* (left), and the *Mountbatten family*, both large land-owners in the area.

Middle section

The mock-gothic *parish church of St John*, Rownhams, is on the left. This was built in 1856 for the new parish created from parts of Nursling and Chilworth.

The River Test at Mottisfont

Mottisfont Abbey gardens

Rownhams House (top right) is the only surviving example of many large middle-class residences built for Southampton businesssmen in the second half of the 18th century. Below it is *Ivy Cottage*, one of the oldest houses in the area, probably dating from the 16th century. Between it and the church is the *radio mast* erected on top of an underground reservoir at Toothill. The line below the church and Ivy Cottage represents the M27.

The popular *Romsey Golf Course* is shown on the left and to its right is *Grove Place*, a splendid Elizabethan mansion built for John Paget between 1565 and 1585. At one time it served as a lunatic asylum, and in World War II it was an American base. In 1961 it was converted into a boys' boarding school named Northcliffe School.

© Crown copyright licence no. LA079715

In the bottom right corner is *St Boniface Church*, Nursling, an early 14th century decorated style country church with evidence of an earlier, possibly Saxon, building. To its left is the only surviving *mill* in Nursling. A plaque on the wall records that it was built in 1728 on a frame of large beech timbers given by Sir Richard Mill. Behind it is a *pylon*, one of many which dominate the skyline. The *phragmites reed* and the *spotted*

orchid are examples of plants in the Lower Test Reserve, established in 1978.

Lower border

An *oak branch*, symbolising the sacred oak of pagan German tribes which, according to legend, was chopped down by Boniface; a *salmon*; *hazel nuts*, a reference to the name Nutshalling; a *green woodpecker*, once common but becoming rarer.

Nursling

EAST TYTHERLEY

East Tytherley is the smallest village in Test Valley and one of the smallest in Hampshire. Its old English name suggests that it was a 'little place with water and pasturage', a description which still holds good. In 1335 Edward III gave Tytherley to Queen Philippa who sought refuge there with her court when London was afflicted with the plague. Sadly, two of her courtiers were already infected and soon they and three-quarters of the villagers had died.

Top border

The *five butterflies* were described at the time as 'local' but sadly the designer of the panel has since died and neither her notes nor her drawings survive. A local naturalist is unable to identify the first, which appears to be a moth, but suggests that, allowing for some artistic licence, the other four could be: small tortoiseshell; swallowtail; orange tip; small copper.

Middle section

The *parish church of St Peter* replaced an earlier building in the middle of the 13th century, and remained almost unaltered until 1863 when the porch, transept and vestry were added. Thirty years later the tower was built. The giant *yew tree* was planted by Denys Rolle, Lord of the Manor from 1755.

Behind the church is a field of *oil-seed rape*. Next to the church is the attractive timbered *Letterbox Cottage* with its comparatively rare Victorian letter box. Above it hovers a *kestrel*, one of several birds of prey which nest locally. The Manor was acquired by Sir Francis Rolle in 1672. *Rolle House*, below Letterbox Cottage, was established in 1718 by Sarah Rolle as a charity school, one of the earliest in England, 'for four poor boys and six poor girls. . . to be decently clothed in blue . . . to have a halfpenny loaf of brown bread and a halfpenny worth of cheese every day that they should come to school . . . .' Her charity still benefits local children. Rolle House is now a private residence. On the right is the stump of a *tulip tree* partially blown down in the 1987 gale.

The *Star Inn* is splendidly represented in the bottom left corner. Within living memory one of two shops in the village was located in The Star. Although neither shop survives, the skittle alley in the pub is a popular rendezvous. The *sheep* in the park and the *cows* in the foreground represent local farming activities.

Lower border

The *village name* and a charming little *mouse*.

Sheep in Tytherley Park

**Michelmersh
Braishfield
Lockerley**

MICHELMERSH, BRAISHFIELD and LOCKERLEY

© Crown copyright licence no. LA079715

Michelmersh Church

MICHELMERSH

Michelmersh is a scattered village spread out on high ground which drops down to the Test on the far side of the A3057 Stockbridge to Romsey Road. In 985 King Athelred granted the village its charter, the millenium of which was celebrated enthusiastically in 1985.

Top border

Queen Emma, who presented the Manor of Michelmersh to St. Swithun at Winchester in 1043. On the table beside her is the Michelmersh Pot, a late Saxon pot found intact inside a small kiln discovered in a garden at Haccups Point in the late 1970s; the *archer and mounted knight* refer to the tradition that in 1415 more than six hundred knights and archers camped in the parish before setting sail for France and the Battle of Agincourt. The field is still known as Agincourt Field; the *gentleman on the black horse* is Sir William Ogle who defended Winchester Castle for the King against Cromwell in 1645. His second wife Sarah, owned Manor Farm in Michelmersh. Legend has it that his ghostly carriage is heard in the lanes at night; the *soldier on sentry duty* and the *army truck* represent the

units, including Canadian forces, which camped here before the D-day invasion of Normandy; the *bricks* are those still made from local clay.

Middle section

In the centre at the top is the *parish church* dedicated to 'Our Lady' but known as St Mary's. It is 13th century, probably built on Saxon foundations. Its unusual wooden bell-tower was added in the 15th century. One of the memorials is a cross-legged effigy of a Crusader knight with a stag at his feet. There is also one of Sir William Ogle. To the left is *the barn*, formerly an unusual five-bayed granary, now refurbished and the venue for village activities. Part of the film 'Worzel Gummidge' was made there. *The fields* show local arable farming. Top right is *Michelmersh Court*, which was formerly the Rectory when Michelmersh was one of the richest livings in the country. It is now the family home of Sir David Frost.

The house on the left below the barn is the *Old House*, formerly the Dower House, home of Sir William Ogle and is said to be the destination for his ghost! The yellow bricked house is *Michelmersh House*, originally Michelmersh Farm House and below the *sheep* is *Manor Farm*, the site associated with Queen Emma's gift to Winchester, probably the oldest building in the village.

In the left centre, below the Old House, are *strawberries* at Yew Tree Farm which, with other fruit and vegetables, has long been a popular 'pick-your-own' venue. The *row of cottages* to the right of the strawberry field are houses built for estate workers during the last century. Most have been modernised and extended including the one occupied by Shirley Morrish, the panel's designer. The fine house on the right is *The Old Rectory*. Below the strawberry field is one of the *postwar houses*. To the left of the *red telephone kiosk* is the *Old Bakery* where villagers took their cakes to be cooked. Below the bakery is a *small bungalow*, typical of a number built in the 1930s. At the other side is the *smithy*, happily still functioning with Les Ninnim wielding the hammer and tongs.

In the centre is the *Michelmersh Brick Company*, Britain's largest manufacturer of traditional handmade bricks and roofing tiles. Michelmersh craftsmen have been making bricks with the abundant clay for at least a thousand years. Michelmersh bricks are used in prestigious new buildings and the refurbishment of stately homes all over the country.

The bottom corner features a *stretch of the River Test* which forms the western boundary of the parish, and *cattle* which symbolise local dairy farming. Opposite is the *Bear and Ragged Staff*, the village public house. The signboard bears the coat of arms of the Earls of Warwick because the first Earl was known as the 'Bear' having strangled one single-handed, whilst another is reputed to have slain a giant with a tree-shaped club, hence 'The Bear and Ragged Staff'. At one time it was celebrated for cock fighting but now is renowned for an annual pumpkin competition. In front of the pub is the *Michelmersh Silver Band* which celebrated its centenary in 1985. It was originally formed as a Temperance Band and at least one village family has had an unbroken relationship with it since its formation.

Lower border

A *willow tree*; two *swallows* and a *swan* found in the lower part of the village; the *village name* surrounded by some of the flowers which grow there. The right hand side has a *barn owl*, a *deer* and an *oak tree* for the higher part of the village.

A laid hedge at Timsbury

Michelmersh brickworks

BRAISHFIELD

Braishfield, formerly part of Michelmersh, is not mentioned in the Domesday Book, but the parish contains a number of prehistoric settlement sites and a probable Roman villa. The present straggling village is a tasteful combination of old and new.

Top border

Mesolithic Man. Excavations were started on Broom Hill in 1971 by Michael O'Malley, a keen archaeologist who spent several summers working alone on the isolated hilltop. He surveyed what was described as 'a combination of an Iron Age round house with an Anglo Saxon sunken hut', and recovered over 89,000 worked flints, the largest Later Mesolithic find from a British site; a separate excavation on nearby *Fern Hill* carried out by volunteers of the Lower Test Valley Archaeological Study Group under the direction of Kevin Stubbs from 1975 to 1979 uncovered the remains of a Roman bath house, apparently built in the late third or early 4th century AD; the *oak tree*, the village emblem, stands in the school grounds; the *red coat soldier* and the flags represent the semaphore station known to have been one of a chain during the

The monument at Farley Mount

Napoleonic period; in the vestry at Farley Chamberlayne Church, hung high in the rafters, is a *cresset beacon* which could date from the reign of Edward III, used at Farley Mount at the time of the *Armada* when a signal of fire stretched across the land gave warning of the approach of the Spanish fleet.

Middle section

The large house at the top is *Braishfield Manor*, built as a farm house in 1550 and known then as Pitt House. It was enlarged in 1760 and in this century new wings were added. During the 1920s and 1930s Mrs Maude King, a famous breeder of hackney ponies, and her husband Alfred lived at The Manor. Mrs King was a great benefactress to the village, presenting the school with a recreation ground and regularly entertaining village children at Christmas. In the other corner is the *memorial on Farley Mount* featured also in the King's Somborne panel.

To the lower right is the red brick *parish church of All Saints*, built only in 1855. The bell tower and clock were added in 1902 to commemorate the Coronation of King Edward VII. To the left of the parish church is the *United Reformed Church*, built in 1818 as a Congregational Chapel and enlarged in

1906. It became the United Reformed Church in 1971 on the union of the Congregational Church with the Presbyterians. In the centre of the panel is the *imposing war memorial*.

The *village pond* on the right, with *children* playing on the banks, has since been dredged and relined. The *willow tree* is no longer there, but *children* regularly feed the resident ducks and moorhens. Below the pond is *the school*, built by the Michelmersh School Board in 1876 with a new extension, built in the Victorian style to blend in with the original, called the Elizabeth Sheppard wing in memory of a very popular headteacher. *Children* play netball in the playground. Below and to the left of the United Reformed Church is a *scarecrow*, recalling that Pucknell Farm in the parish was used as 'Scatterbrook Farm' for the television series 'Worzel Gummidge' starring Jon Pertwee.

The public house is the *Newport Inn*.

In the bottom left corner is a remarkable village character *Reginald Guy (Boxer) Old* with his steam tractor *'Boxer's Beauty'*. Boxer's whole life was spent in agriculture. In the days before combine harvesters Boxer and his father Walter went from farm to farm with their threshing tackle: engine; threshing machine, water cart, elevator and caravan. In his later years he went, with Beauty, to many steam rallies. He died in 1980 and his coffin was taken to church on a trailer pulled by Beauty.

Lower border

Representative plant life: *ragged robin*, *cedar tree* (several grow in the gardens of the larger houses); *cowslip*; *wild orchid*; *bluebell* and *foxgloves*.

Braishfield pond

Romany gypsy caravan

Parish Church of St John, Lockerley

LOCKERLEY

Lockerley, a scattered village with four greens, lies in the valley of the River Dun which joins the Test at Dunbridge. The area would have been known to travellers on the ancient Ridgeway along Dean Hill and Tope Hill five thousand years ago. By 1000 BC there was a settlement at Canefield where Bronze Age pottery was discovered in 1940.

Top border

In the centre is the *Victoria Cross* won on 26th August 1914 (one of the earliest in the War) by Bombardier Fred Luke who lived at Lockerley Green and who served with the 37th Battery Field Artillery at Le Cateau when the battery was overrun by Germans and two guns were lost. Fred and two companions managed to retrieve one of the guns under heavy fire and all three were awarded the V.C; on either side are *trout* found in the River Dun.

Middle section

The design is based on the four village greens. At the top left is *Top Green*, the highest, surrounded by a mixture of *old and modern houses*. In the top centre is *Dean Hill*, while top right is *Holbury* where there is still a mill by the river. Running diagonally across the panel is a stretch of the *railway line* that runs from Salisbury through Romsey to Portsmouth, with a busy station at Dunbridge. On the left, below Top Green, is *Lockerley Post Office*, while the *yellow faced building* on the right is the *village stores*. Both play an important part in the communal life of the village. Below the stores are the man-made *Lockerley Ponds*, created to provide commercial fishing facilities. The *River Dun* runs under the *ancient mill*, now a private residence.

On the right of the river is the *parish church of St John the Evangelist*. For a short time Lockerley had two churches side by side as the present church was consecrated on 16th October 1890 while the ancient church was not demolished until the following year. Stones are set in the ground to denote the exact position of the old church and daffodils mark the lines of the walls. The new church was built by Frederick Dalgety, at a cost of between £6,000 and £7,000, with timber for the pews and the chancel ceiling coming from forests in New Zealand owned by the Dalgety family, squires of Lockerley from Tudor times.

Below the cornfield on the left is the *school* and next to it the *village hall*. After the formation of the Lockerley Hall Estate in the mid 18th century the pressing need for a school in the village was met by the generosity of Frederick Dalgety and another landowner, Sir Francis Goldsmid. The school was opened in 1871 and still meets the needs of local primary school children. The village hall was also given to the village by the Dalgety family after the First World War. The school and hall face on to *Butts Green*, so called because of its links with archery and used for the village fete, various sports and social gatherings.

Critchells' Green is a little off the beaten track and is rather more wild than the others. *Critchells' farm house*, shown at the bottom, is one of the oldest houses in the village, built probably in the 16th century.

Lower border

This shows birds quite common near the river and around the area – *swans*, *moorhens* and *Canada geese*.

Holbury Mill, Lockerley

Awbridge
Sherfield English
Wellow

Awbridge

SHERFIELD ENGLISH   WELLOW

AWBRIDGE, SHERFIELD ENGLISH and WELLOW

© Crown copyright licence no. LA079715

AWBRIDGE

As an ecclesiastical parish, Awbridge (pronounced Aybridge) is comparatively new, having been carved out of surrounding parishes in the 1870s. The civil parish is even newer having been part of Sherfield English parish until 1984. The name Awbridge derives from Abedric as in the Domesday Book, which by the 12th century had become Abrigg, or 'Abbot's ridge'.

Top border

The school. This was opened as a Board School in 1877 and with all such schools it was attended by pupils of all ages until the early 1950s when, it became a 5-11 years Primary School. The school now serves a wide area, drawing pupils from Sherfield English, Michelmersh, Timsbury, Newtown, Carters Clay and, of course, Awbridge itself, with, currently, 150 pupils on roll. The school recently won a Hampshire Schools' Garden award for the development of a knot garden based on a Tudor design; *All Saints Church*: until the church was built in 1885/86 (of brick and Swanage stone in Gothic style at a cost of £2,800) parishioners had to walk to Michelmersh for Services. The greater part of the cost of All Saints was subscribed

Awbridge School

by the Rev T H Tragett. There is just one bell. An extension was built in 1993.

Middle section

Awbridge is a loosely connected series of hamlets with the main population centred around *Kents Oak* which dominates the panel. This prominent, magnificent, tree is probably several centuries old. The *high ground* in the panel denotes the hilly nature of the parish, with Abbot's Ridge in mind. The *tractor* on the left in the ploughed field symbolises the agricultural nature of the locality while *the golfer*, swinging his club on the right, the Dunwood Manor Golf Course between Awbridge and Sherfield English. The golf course is in Danes Road, a name which recalls the troubled times of the Danish occupation. There is a fort, probably Danish, just outside the parish boundary.

There are several trout lakes in the area but *the lake* in the panel behind Kents Oak is at Awbridge Danes. This was created in the 1920s to provide work for the local unemployed, each man receiving one shilling (5p) a day and a loaf of bread.

The *Friesian cow and calf* on the right of the tree and *the chickens* on the left represent

local dairy and egg farming. The rather unusual four-sided *parish notice board* was presented to the newly formed Parish Council in 1984 by the equally newly formed Community Association. Soaring into the sky above the tree is a *hot air balloon* owned by a local enthusiast, Mr Barker. The balloon was a familiar sight, taking off from the golf course.

Lower border

Rhododendrons representing the many banks of shrubs to be seen in the locality; *mushrooms*, from the local mushroom farm, an important employer of part time workers.

Awbridge

Rhododendrons

Sherfield English Church

Dunwood Manor Golf Club

SHERFIELD ENGLISH

Sherfield English is one of the parishes to the west of Romsey and reaches the Wiltshire border. It has many of the characteristics of the New Forest and its flora, with larger and older trees and denser undergrowth than the rest of Test Valley.

It is a small village along the A27, Romsey to Salisbury road with little more than the church, the Hatchet Inn, the village hall, a garage and a few houses to catch the eye of the speeding motorist. Many of its cottages and lonely farms are located down narrow, winding lanes. At the time of the Domesday Book the name was Sirefelle which by the 16th century had become Shervill. The name English derives from the l'Engleys family. It is not known when the family became tenants of the manor but Gilbert l'Engleys held land in the neighbourhood as early as 1254 and Richard l'Engleys is mentioned in 14th century documents.

Top border

Shield of Smith of Ellingham. Bartholomew Smith bought the estate in 1629 from the Tichborne family but continued to lease it to them. The last member of the family to hold it was Henry Lockhard Smith who sold it to Louisa Lady Ashburton in 1903; *shield of the l'Engleys* referred to above; *shield of Ringwood family*. In 1428 the manor was acquired by Thomas Ringwood and was held by the family until 1566.

Middle section

The panel was designed to depict a representative scene in springtime through the hills with the *church* dominating the picture as it does the parish. The church, dedicated to St Leonard, is the third to stand in the village. The first was about a quarter of a mile north of the site of the present church. The second was built in 1858 by the Rev the Hon F Baring but was pulled down in 1902-03 on the grounds that it was unsafe. The present church was given to the village in 1903 by Lady Ashburton in memory of her only child Mary Florence, Marchioness of Northampton, who died in 1902. The tall, spired church built of red brick with stone dressings, with its square tower, flying buttresses and pinnacles, is a local landmark. The interior is rich in detail with art nouveau glass in the windows. The church has an impressive peal of 8 bells. In the bottom left hand corner is part of the *old churchyard and wall*. To its right is the *path to the church* through *daffodil and bluebell woods*, with specimen trees and typical wild flowers in grass and gravel.

Lower border

Hedgerow fruits – *brambles* and *rosehips*.

WELLOW

Wellow was once two parishes separated by the River Blackwater, East Wellow in Hampshire and West Wellow in Wiltshire. In 1895 the county boundary was moved and West Wellow was brought into Hampshire and the two combined to form the parish of Wellow. Its origins go back to at least 825 when King Alfred left 'the toune of Welewe' in his will to his eldest daughter Ethelgifu. In the Domesday Book 'Welue' was held by Agemund who had five 'hides' of about 600 acres there. In 1251 Henry III granted a charter to Wellow to hold an annual fair on the eve of St Margaret's Day, probably in the neighbourhood of St Margaret's Church.

St Margaret's church, East Wellow

Top border

Shield of the Gurnays. West Wellow, then in Wiltshire, was held by Robert de Gurnay from about 1240. He died in 1269 and the manor passed to his grandson John. In 1296 it was settled under the name of Wellow Gurnay on John de Badenham; the *Parish Council medallion* worn by the Chairman. It was made in 1987 by a local jewellery designer Lionel Pepper, and paid for by public subscription; the *arms of the Berkeley family*.

The manor probably came into the possession of Thomas de Berkeley from John de Badenham in 1330. It was held by the family until 1494.

Middle section

The *country scene* at the top of the panel represents the farming activities in the area. The bright yellow *oil seed rape*, which attracted a subsidy, became a popular crop during the 1980s. Prominent on the left is the *Sounding Arch* which carried a carriage driveway over the road below to Embley Park, home of Florence Nightingale's family. As the archway was in a deep cutting noises echoed under the arch, children shouting, horses' hooves and later farm machinery, giving rise to the name. As part of a road widening scheme the arch was demolished. A seat made from some of the stones stands near the site of the old arch. In the past tales were told of ghostly carriages passing over the arch at midnight on New Year or Christmas nights. To the right of the arch are *rhododendron bushes* in Ryedown Lane.

In the bottom left hand corner *New Forest ponies* graze amid gorse and heather on *Canada Common*. There is considerable speculation regarding the origins of the

name. One theory is that the area reminded someone of Canada.

More plausible is the theory that this part of Wellow was being inhabited at the time people were being encouraged to seek their fortunes in Canada. The settlers could claim land on the common by erecting a dwelling of some sort between dawn and dusk and having smoke coming from a chimney by dusk, a system apparently used by settlers in Canada. The name Canada appeared on maps early this century, which discounts yet another theory, that Canadian troops stationed there during the First World War gave it the name. The truth is that no one really knows. *The trees* in the panel are some of the many growing in the parish.

Prominent on the right is the *church of St Margaret of Antioch* in East Wellow. The church was started in the year of Magna Carta and completed in 1216 and is built of flint with stone facings and a tiled roof. The door is full of nail holes where rats and other vermin had been nailed until paid for by the church wardens. Outstanding are the remains of wall paintings discovered under thick coats of whitewash in 1891 and thought to date from 1270. Fixed to one of the chancel beams is an ancient musket, placed

Canada Common

there as a warning against the careless use of firearms after the accidental killing of a maidservant by another servant.

The church is visited by people, especially nurses, from all over the world to see the tomb of Florence Nightingale, the famous Crimean nurse known as the 'Lady of the Lamp' and among mementos at the church is a lamp. Florence lived with her family at Embley Park. She died in Park Lane in London and her body was brought back to Wellow to be buried in the family vault. Her *memorial stone* is at the bottom of the panel. It is a plainly designed pyramidal monument with the very simple inscription below a cross: 'F.N. Born 15 May 1820 Died 13 August 1910.' This was strictly in accordance with her wishes. F.N. was how she always signed herself in her later years.

Lower border

Rose hips and *brambles*.

The Florence Nightingale memorial at East Wellow

Romsey
Romsey Extra

ROMSEY and ROMSEY EXTRA

© Crown copyright licence no. LA079715

There is evidence that there was some form of Romano-British settlement in Romsey, which developed on the gravel terrace surrounded by streams and skirted by the River Test to the west of the town. The Old English 'ey' means 'island' or 'raised area in marshland' as here. The element 'Rum' is from a personal name. The river crossing, now called Middlebridge, acted as a focus with roads from Southampton, Salisbury, Stockbridge and Winchester.

It was to the Abbey, however, that Romsey owed its prosperity. It seems there was a religious community by about the eighth century and certainly by the tenth a large community of nuns lived and worshipped on the present Abbey site. In AD 907 King Edward the Elder apparently gave the nuns a great deal of land and encouraged the highest and wealthiest in the land to join the community. King Alfred's grand-daughter, Aethelflaeda, became the first Abbess. The town of Romsey flourished with all the business engendered by the Abbey, with its rich farmlands, its building works, the weekly market and two trade fairs under its patronage each year.

The river Test also contributed to the town's development, attracting mills. At Domesday there were three mills at Romsey and the ready availability of water attracted others – for fulling cloth as well as grinding corn, for making paper, parchment and leather board. The river also led to other industries such as tanning and brewing. The Abbey still stands guardian over the town as it has for a thousand years but many may owe their recognition of Romsey to the glimpses of its streets and buildings seen in the Ruth Rendell 'Inspector Wexford' TV series, filmed in the town.

The parish which surrounds the town of Romsey (or Romsey Infra as it was known) is Romsey Extra.

View over Romsey

Top border

Shields of individuals and families connected with Romsey's history:

1 – *St Aethelflaeda*;

2 – *Pauncefoot*: The family held the manor which bore their name from the start of the 13th century to 1521;

3 – *Ashley family*. The Hon Anthony Evelyn Melbourne Ashley inherited the manor of Romsey Infra from his uncle, Lord Mount Temple of Mount Temple (Co Sligo) in 1888;

4 – *St Barbe* 1605 to 1723: in 1607 King James I stayed at Broadlands as a guest of Edward and Frances St Barbe. He planted a mulberry tree in the grounds and gave Borough status to Romsey Infra. There is a fine monument to the St Barbe family in Romsey Abbey;

5 – *Portman*: The manor of Pauncefoot Hill was bought by Sir Henry Portman in 1588 and it was held by his family until 1680;

6 – the *arms of Romsey*;

7 – *Romsey* 1299 to 1537;

8 – *Palmerston*: The first Lord Palmerston bought Broadlands in 1726 and when the third Lord, the eminent statesman, died, in 1865, it passed to his stepson, William Cowper Temple;

9 – *Fleming*: The family acquired the manor of Romsey Infra in 1679, holding it until 1736;

10 – *Sir William Petty*: He was born in Romsey on 26th May 1623 and from humble beginnings he achieved great wealth and rank, and was a founder member of the Royal Society. Whilst teaching anatomy at Oxford he received the body of a hanged murderess, Anne Green, planning to use it for dissection. But he found that she was still alive, and when she recovered he exhibited the poor wretch. He died in December 1687 and there is a 19th century effigy of him in Romsey Abbey.

11 – the *badge designed by Prince Albert* and presented by Queen Victoria to Florence Nightingale in 1855, recognising her services in the Crimean War.

Middle section

Dominating the panel, as it does the town, is the beautiful and historic *Abbey Church of St Mary and St Aethelflaeda*. A church was first built here in AD 907 by Edward the Elder. The Abbey was developed on Benedictine lines by King Edgar and was sacked by the Danes in 1004. It was rebuilt. There was a second rebuilding in 1120 which took 110

Details of Romsey Abbey

Statue of Lord Palmerston

years to complete. The present church, which dates from that time, is undoubtedly one of the finest Norman buildings in Europe. It has been said: 'It is music in stone'.

The Abbey was badly hit by the Black Death of 1349. Most of the nuns and their servants died and although they struggled back to some sort of normality, it was never the same. Some of the later Abbesses brought the Abbey into disrepute, gaining a bad reputation for laxity, eating, drinking, gossiping and bad language, spending the night in town or staying late in bed!

In 1539 Romsey's monastic community was dissolved. The convent buildings to the south were demolished but the Church was saved, as the townspeople had no other church. The suppressed Abbey was sold to the people of the town in 1544 for £100. In 1994 a programme of concerts, exhibitions and special events marked the 450th anniversary of the preservation of the Abbey.

There is plenty of interest inside the Abbey, including medieval wall paintings, a Saxon rood, 14th century tiles and modern tapestries. Thousands now visit the Abbey to view the grave of Lord Mountbatten, whose home was nearby Broadlands.

Top left is *Broadlands* in its 400 acre park on either side of the Test to the south of the town. Broadlands is actually in the Romsey Extra parish. Its magnificent site near the river is enhanced by the lawns and trees and you can see one of the magnificent *oaks* in the upper left corner. After the dissolution of the monasteries Broadlands passed into the ownership of the St Barbe family and then, in 1736, it was acquired by Henry Temple, the first Lord Palmerston. He enlarged the house and had the grounds laid out by Capability Brown whose son-in-law, Henry Holland, remodelled the interior. The first two Palmerstons, both collectors, enriched the house with works of art. The third Lord Palmerston, who became the Victorian Prime Minister and is remembered for his gunboat diplomacy, was born in Broadlands in 1784 and inherited it in 1801 at the age of 17. His public life kept him away from his Hampshire home for long periods, a source of regret. Later, the estate passed to Colonel Wilfred Ashley, who, on elevation to the peerage, revived the title of Mount Temple, and on his death to his daughter, Edwina, who married Lord Louis Mountbatten, later Earl Mountbatten of Burma. In the 1950s Lady Mountbatten did much to restore the house to its 18th century elegance.

The Queen and Prince Philip spent part of their honeymoon in 1947 at Broadlands as did Prince Charles and Lady Diana Spencer in 1981. In 1979, only months before the murder of Lord Mountbatten by the IRA, the house was opened to the public, his nephew Prince Charles performing the ceremony. Lord Mountbatten's eldest grandson, Lord Romsey, inherited the estate and now lives there.

Behind Broadlands is *Green Hill* with its splendid view of the Abbey, dwarfing the rest of the town, a location much favoured by artists and photographers. To the right is *Saddlers Mill* with the bridge where, in October, salmon can be seen jumping as they migrate upstream for spawning. Special padding and fencing are erected to protect the fish from injury.

Across the Test, in the bottom left hand corner, is the fine statue by Matthew Noble of *Lord Palmerston* which stands in the centre of the square in the town. To the right is the row of *modern houses* overlooking the Abbey Green while between those houses and the Abbey is *King John's House* and the *Tudor Cottage*, situated off Church Street. A popular tradition is that it was used as a hunting lodge by King John in 1210 – five years

before Magna Carta – but there is no evidence. A document of Henry III records that he granted to the Abbess of Romsey Abbey a hunting lodge built by his father, King John, but there is no positive connection with the house in question. Followers of Edward I certainly stayed there in 1306 whilst he was visiting the Abbess and we know it was used as an isolation hospital during the Black Death. During the Civil War the building was used as a billet for soldiers and in 1781 it became Romsey's first workhouse.

Now, after restoration, the complex is open to the public for part of the year and the refurbished Tudor garden was opened to the public during 1995.

In the centre foreground is *Linden House* in The Hundred, which, with many other places in the town, has been used as a location for the Inspector Wexford television series.

Right of the Abbey is *Romsey Town Hall*, purpose-built for the needs of the Corporation in the 1860s on the south side of the Market Place and now occupied by the Romsey Town Council. Lord Palmerston helped finance the project which

Broadlands

also attracted a government grant as it incorporated the County Court. He did not live to see its opening in 1866.

Below the Town Hall is *Strong's Brewery*, established by David Faber, a member of the banking and publishing family. He bought the three largest breweries in the town, all in a poor state, and built up a very successful business under the name of Strongs. Railway travellers were informed, 'You are in the Strong Country', on railside hoardings, and in the town the sign was, 'The heart of the Strong Country'. Strong's became part of Whitbread in the 1960s and the brewing side ceased in 1980. The site has been redeveloped for offices and houses.

The train, centre right, represents the lines from Eastleigh and Southampton which converge on Romsey. Above the train is the *Sounding Arch*, strictly in Wellow parish, which connected two parts of the Embley Estate and here represents the many bridges in Romsey.

The trees in the top right hand corner are at the world famous *Sir Harold Hillier Arboretum* between Ampfield and Braishfield. Hilliers was founded in 1864 by Edwin Hillier who had trained as a plantsman and who bought

a small florist and nursery business in Winchester. The business flourished under his sons and, in due course, his grandson Harold, who, like his father and grandfather, was an avid plant collector. In June 1953, the day after the Coronation, Harold and his wife moved into Jermyns House and the project which was to grow into an internationally known plant collection was begun. Twenty-five years later, in May 1978, Queen Elizabeth the Queen Mother attended the opening of the Arboretum, accepting it on behalf of Hampshire County Council. Sir Harold gave his collection to the County to be held by them in perpetuity as a charitable trust. After his death in 1985, Lady Hillier gave Jermyns House as well to the County Council and the Arboretum and gardens now extend to more than 150 acres of world renown. The Arboretum is open to the public and guided tours take place in all seasons.

Tucked in the bottom right hand corner is the little *church of St Swithun's*, Crampmoor, built in 1858 to serve a rural community as a school-church. Before 1858 services were occasionally held at a Dame School on Halterworth Hill, or, more often, in the 'large room' at the home of Mrs James Feltham of New Pond. 'Squire' Fleming

15th/16th century manor house in Palmerston Street

gave the land for the school on the proviso that church services were held there each Sunday. On weekdays the chancel was shut off by wooden panelling. The teacher's house was entered by a door in the south wall where the lectern now stands. At weekends all evidence of the school was packed away, the room thoroughly scrubbed and the panelling removed to reveal the sanctuary in readiness for Sunday services. After evensong the process was reversed. A new school was built in 1927 in School Road, behind the Hunters Inn.

Over the years many improvements have taken place and St Swithun's, a daughter church of Romsey Abbey, is still a cherished building with a service every Sunday morning.

Among the wildlife to be seen at the bottom of the panel are: *kingfisher, redshank, longtailed tit, mallard, rosebay willowherb* and an *owl*.

Lower border

Marsh marigold; *poppy*; *dog rose*; *bind weed*; *meadow cranesbill*; *harebell*.

The Horsefair

Saddler's Mill

North Baddesley
Ampfield
Chilworth

NORTH BADDESLEY   AMPFIELD   CHILWORTH

NORTH BADDESLEY, AMPFIELD and CHILWORTH

© Crown copyright licence no. LA079715

St John's, North Baddesley

NORTH BADDESLEY

North Baddesley, although still a village, has many of the features of a small town with a parish population exceeding 9000. In 1921 it was fewer than 400 but by the outbreak of war in 1939 it was almost 1000. Its proximity to Southampton and Eastleigh gave rise to considerable pressure for development after the war and large estates of modern houses were built. The most recent of the parish's developments is Valley Park, Chandler's Ford, which straddles the border of Test Valley and Eastleigh Boroughs.

The name Baddesley (Old English 'Baeddes Leah' or 'Baeddi's woodland') marked the northern and southern extremities of the New Forest, South Baddesley being near Lymington.

Top border

In the centre is the *badge of the Parish Council Chairman*. The *shields* include The *Knights of St. John of Jerusalem*. The medieval Knights Hospitallers of St John established their headquarters at Baddesley following the Black Death in the 14th Century. They

remained until the Dissolution when they suffered with other religious orders. Other shields are of *Fleming*, Lords of the Manor from 1600; *Chamberlayne*, Lords from 1781; *Mortimer*, held lands from 1086.

Middle section

In the upper centre is the *parish church of St John the Baptist*, reputedly built on the site of a pagan temple. It stands at the highest point of a long narrow ridge running east-west. Parts date from the 14th century, the list of incumbents commencing in 1304. In the chancel is a rare Bible of 1620.

The *chimney* (top left) marks the chemical factory of *Borden (UK) Ltd*, established in 1947. It employs around 300 people and produces a range of goods including adhesives and cling film. Below it is the *Manor House* which was built on the site of the Hospitallers' headquarters, of which the Manor's cellars were probably part. The 16th century building was probably quad-rangular around a well in the kitchen court but the present is mainly 18th century. The *White Cottage* (top right) is one of the few remaining houses of corrugated iron built after World War I. The area was dubbed 'Tin town 'twixt Rownhams and Romsey'.

Below the Manor House is the *Roman Catholic Church*, consecrated in April 1975. Before that, Catholics worshipped at St Joseph's Convent Chapel in Romsey. The first Mass was celebrated by Bishop Derek Warlock. Opposite the church is the *Bede's Lea public house*.

The large white building in the centre foreground is the *headquarters of builders Hall and Tawse*, formerly the factory for Reema prefabricated buildings. Below are a number of plants found in Emer Bog, a 60 acre reserve owned and managed by the Hampshire Wildlife Trust and part of a Site of Special Scientific Interest. The plants are: *willow*, *water horsetail*, *water avens*, *marsh marigold*, *southern marsh orchid* with a background of *sedges* and *reeds*.

Lower border

Fallow deer; *fungi*; a *warbler*, a *purple emperor butterfly*.

AMPFIELD

Ampfield derives its name from the spring which rises near the church. The earliest name was 'An felde', 'an' being the Celtic word for a spring.

Top border

The *Gospel Oak with a copy of the Bible underneath*. This ancient tree marked the boundary of the parish with North Baddesley and it was here the annual 'beating the bounds' procession at Rogationtide would halt for a reading of a portion from the Gospels; the *quill and inkpot* represent Richard Morley the 'hedge poet'. His family owned land at 'Anfield' and Richard went to school in Baddesley. He died in 1672 and was buried in Hursley; the *arms of the Heathcote family*, five generations of landowners from 1718; *pottery*, symbolising a traditional village industry. *Bloody Bridge* in Jermyns Lane. The legend says that Cynegils, the first Christian King of Wessex was murdered here in 643 AD, probably by the forces of Edwin, King of Northumbria.

Knapp Wood, Ampfield

Ampfield House

Middle section

At the top is *Ampfield House*, built in 1760 by Joseph White. In 1902 the house and estate were bought by the publishing family of Faber and later acquired by Hillier Nurseries as their headquarters.

To the right of the house is the *Women's Institute hall*. To the left and below is the village *post-office stores* with the *red telephone kiosk*. Since the tapestry was worked the shop has closed.

The thatched, half timbered building in the centre is the *Elizabethan barn* at Hawkstead Farm, reputedly once the headquarters of a gang of smugglers. Below the barn is *Wooley Pond* through which the village boundary with Braishfield passes. In former times local youths would wade through the pond, duck underneath the dividing chain and emerge on the other side to claim a kiss from the waiting girls. At the bottom left is *St Andrews Church* known affectionately as 'the church in the woods'. Ampfield became a parish only in 1841 and St Mark's Day that year saw the dedication of the church on the site chosen by John Keble of Hursley. The ceremony was attended by leading members of the Oxford Group.

To the right of the barn is the 'old' *Potters Heron hotel*, built on the site of the old pottery. A Potter's treadle wheel was known as a 'hern' because of its dipping movement, and 'hern' is an old name for a heron. Nearby, are some of the *clay pits*. Below is one of the oldest houses in Ampfield, '*Mrs Topping's Cottage*'. To the left can be seen the sign of the *White Horse public house*, *Ampfield Primary School* and the *War Memorial*.

At the bottom is *The Straight Mile*, a very attractive stretch of the Romsey-Winchester road; bounded by trees many of which were purchased by local subscriptions to save them from developers. In the bottom right corner is *Thomas the Tank Engine* whose creator, the Rev. W. Awdry, lived in the village as a boy when his father was vicar of St Marks.

Lower border

Badger; thrush; trout and *dog roses*.

CHILWORTH

The village, referred to as Celeworda at Domesday, is now in two parts, modern Chilworth lying along the tree-lined, straight 'new' stretch of the Southampton to Romsey road, and old Chilworth built around the 'old' road.

Top border

A *Roman soldier*; the *Fleming Coat of Arms*. John Fleming acquired Chilworth Manor in 1827; *Chilworth Manor* which was sold to Southampton University in 1967 and converted into a hall of residence. In 1982 there was further major development with the construction of the prestigious Business and Science and Technology complex; *Tower of the Winds*. This was built in 1854/55 by Henry Lucas, an eccentric artist, sculptor and writer as a residence and studio. It was 100ft long and 60ft high but was demolished in 1955; *brick kiln*, many of the bricks used in modern Southampton were manufactured here.

Middle section

In the upper right corner is the *parish church of St Denys*. Of Norman origin, it had become very dilapidated by the beginning of the 19th century and was rebuilt in 1812 by the Lord of the Manor, Peter Serle, at his own expense. The church is noted for its bells, about 800 years old and probably the oldest in Hampshire. Below the church is the *post-office stores*. Originally built to house the squire's hounds, it became the post office in 1900. To its left, *a rider* can be seen negotiating a jump at the riding school. The tiny *War Memorial* is in the centre and to the right are the *Beehive Cottages* on either side of the drive leading to the Manor. In the bottom left corner is the *Clump Inn* whose name derives from the old earthwork, 301 feet high, on which one of the ancient beacon warnings was located. *The pots* in the foreground represent the Manor Farm Pottery.

Lower border

Deer; *fox*; *rabbits*; *squirrel* and *hedgehog*.

St Denys, Chilworth

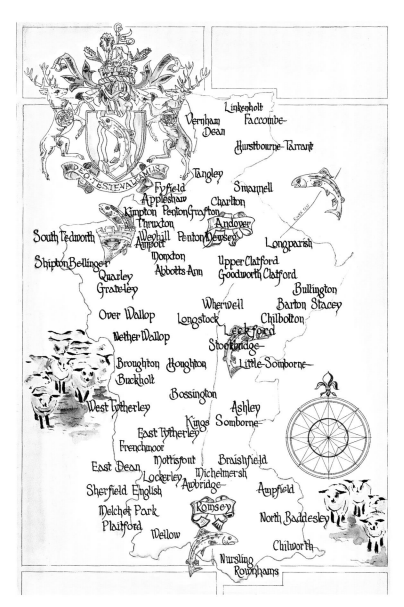

Original design for the Borough map in the Stockbridge panel, painted by Robina Orchard

ACKNOWLEDGEMENTS

Research, Introduction and Tapestry descriptions	Cyril Pigott
Personal overview on execution of Tapestry	Robina Orchard
Editor	Annie Bullen
History Editor	David Allen
Coordinator	Nigel Sacree
Word Processing	Lynn Hellyer and Stephanie Kelly
Design, BAS Printers	Sue Malin

Photographic Credits

Pages 2 and 3	Andover Advertiser
Pages 90, 92b and 105	The School of Army Aviation
Page 130b	Dunwood Manor Golf Club, Awbridge
Tapestry Photographs and page 53	David Facey
Pages 37, 40, 69a, 74b and 115b	Reg Gillam
Page 24b	Lucinda Green
Pages 18b, 22, 23a, 41, 54, 55, 56b, 57, 64, 69b, 73, 83, 86, 91, 92a, 93, 96, 97b, 99a, 103b, 104b, 111b, 114, 115a and 128	Gordon Gumn
Page 4	Hampshire Museum Service
Pages 5, 30b, 32, 44, 45b, 46, 65b, 80, 82a 85, 130a, 133 and 141b	Ed Hendry
Page 129b	Hillier Gardens and Arboretum
Pages 9 and 11	Needlecraft Magazine
Page 63b	Robina Orchard
Page 45a	Mike Otley
Page 74a	John Randall
Front cover and page 98	Nigel Rigden
Pages 84a and 103a	Nigel Sacree
Pages 121b, 125 and 131	Pat Sillence
Pages 17, 18a, 19, 23b, 24a, 25, 28, 29, 30a, 39, 48, 49, 56a, 60, 61a, 62, 63a, 65a, 72, 76, 77, 82b, 84b, 87, 97a, 99b, 102, 104a, 109, 110, 111a, 116, 117, 120, 121a, 122, 123, 124, 129a, 132, 136, 137, 138, 139, 140, 141a, 144, 145, 146 and 147	Glenda Sims
Pages 33, 38, 61b and 81	John Walsh

All those who contributed to the production of tapestries, including:

1. VERNHAM DEAN, LINKENHOLT, UPTON, FACCOMBE, HURSTBOURNE TARRANT

Robert Ablett, Stephen Ablett, Brenda Allen, Stephanie Allsopp, Joy Anthony, Budgie Austin, Jean Baker, Nicola Blacker, Paul Blacker, Joanne Brock, Rachael Brock, Jill Brotherton, Ben Brown, Bassy Brown, Nigel Brown, Richard Burden, Sara Burden, Joan Butchart, Susan Carter, Lee Catherine, Nick Cherrington, Abigail Cook, Dora Cooke, Clara Cooper, Magnus Cooper, Lee Cox, Cecilia Curtis, Philip Daw, Jodie Daw, Christine Dawe, Andrew Dewey, Daniel Dines, Julia Dodson, Grace Dowse, Kevin Dyer, Eleanor Fairbrother, Tom Fairbrother, Stella Foster, Ethna Foster-Carter, Angela Freer-Smith, John Freer-Smith, Ewan Gibson, George Gomez, Ian Gomez, Basil Goode, Margaret Goode, Kristie Grant, Sammy Grant, Simon Hales, Zoe Hales, John Hamblin, Sarah Harley, Lowenna Harbottle, Joan Harris , Jennifer Hawke, Catherine Hensman, Margaret Herriott, Muriel Hewitt, Nancy Higginbotham, Simon Hillier, Sylvia Hingley, Isobel Hogbin, Patricia Holland, David Holmes, Florence Holmes, Liz Holmes (Design), Polly Hosier, Samantha Humphries, Sarah Humphries, Turner Hume, Hilary Iveson, Nicola Jarvis, Paul Jarvis, Emma Jenkin, Mary Luton, James Maddox, Dot Matheson, Abigail Maw, Muriel May, Stefan May, Alex Menzies, Valerie Middleton, Peter Middleton, Hannah Mills, Verity Mills, Vernham Mills, Pam Moore, Claire Morgan, Paul Noutch, Delia Page, Gill Palmer, Katherine Pattison, Emma Peart, Julia Peart, Richard Peel, Zoe Pocock, Penny Portman, Agnes Rasser, Dot Raynsford, Catty Riley, Matthew Rose, Simon Rose, Charlotte Ross, Victoria Robinson, Susie Rushbridge, Kelly Ryder, Maureen Sargent, Edward Sclater, Margaret Seward, Natasha Shepherd, Andrew Simmon, Mark Simmon, Gemma Slator, Rob Smith, Renee Smith, Clare Smith, Antoinette Spencer, Darren Squire, Craig Storey, Andrew Strong, Nicola Strong, Wendy Terry, Guy Terry, Mark Terry, June Vining, Jame Wood, Matthew Watkins, Helen Wurzer, Matthew Withycombe, James Withycombe, Beverley Warne, Jonathon Walker, Paul Wallington, Joanne Winson.

2. TANGLEY, WILDHERN, HATHERDEN, THE APPLESHAWS, PENTON

TANGLEY, WILDHERN, HATHERDEN, Jill Donnelly, Brenda Dunning, Kay Griffin (Design), Susan McGregor, Jan Maynard, Eileen Measures, Marie Spencer, Linda Trueman, Anne Vincent, Denise Wilson, Doreen Winstock; *APPLESHAW,* Valerie Baggallay, Monica Bradley, Delsa Brooks, Barbara Chapman, Alec Clarke (Design), Eileen Clarke, Meg Downs, Winnie Howl, Ursula Merrington, Mary Philpotts, Jane Tarrant; *PENTON,* Jackie Atkinson, Helen Burroughs, Norah Bennett, Nancy Bennett, Elizabeth Dampier-Child, Ann Isherwood, Nancy Kerswill, Mary Lawes, Margaret Linforth (Design), Delphine

Maudsley, Rosemary Moody, Launa Nias, Christine Saunders, Peggy Silburn, Mary Stevens, Florrie Tarrant, Joyce Thorn, Dagma Volkers, Mary Wetherall, Dorothy Williams.

3. CHARLTON, KNIGHTS ENHAM, ENHAM ALAMEIN, SMANNELL

CHARLTON, Ann Berry, Dianne Cammack, Margaret Crossley, Jean Dempster, Margery Levy (Design), Iris Lewis, Linda Peck, Linda Marshall, Brenda Mattick (Design), Liz Newman, Stella Snowden, Joy Taylor; *ENHAM ALAMEIN AND KNIGHTS ENHAM,* Jane Borley, Patricia Borley, Nora Bullen, Renee Bulpit, Brenda Mattick (Design), Julia Reilly (Design), Betty Waters; *SMANNELL,* Sue Armitage, Evelyn Bright, Anne Brook (Design), Phyl Brook, Nora Bullen, Renee Bulpit, Mavis Clarke, Jean Dance, Ruth Davies, Joan Figgins, Joan Gilbert, Sarah Gouriet, Virginia Haines, Vyvyan Hartley, Jennie Humphreys, Susan Joseph, David Jardine, Susan Jardine, Jill Loveridge, Brenda Mattick, Peggy Payne, Gilly Radford, Julia Reilly, Freddie Smith, Margaret Smith, Betty Waters, Peggy White, Henrietta Wood, Pupils of Smannell C of E Primary School.

4. ANDOVER

Elizabeth Acres, Patricia Aitken, Elinor Allan, Gladys Allan, Evelyn Allen, Anne Baker, Dorothy Barlow, Jeanne Birks, Felicia Calin, Daphne Channing, Winnie Daly, Violet Dannatt , Carol Grimstone, Elsie Hayward, Cynthia Jewitt, Niel Jewitt, Rosalyn Lockwood, Meg McConnell, Chris Meads (Design), Lynda Newberry, Morag Painter, Linda Peck, Jean Ross, Elizabeth Rowe, Kathy Rowe, Jean Spurgeon.

5. THRUXTON, FYFIELD, KIMPTON

THRUXTON, Susan Buckmaster, Christine Barrett, Nicola Barrett, Elizabeth Butterworth, Elizabeth Cosgrove, Linda Lilley (Design), Adam Lilley, Rachel Lilley, Hugh McPartlan (Design), Margaret Moylen-Jones, Nora Nash, Frankie Richcord; *FYFIELD,* Cheri Baster, Molly Baster, Win Carr, Jenny Forsyth, Azalea Mayhew (Design), Kathleen Pennells, Augusta Rose, Ann Rowe, John Rowe, Sheila Woodwards, Gillian Yarde-Leavett (Design); *KIMPTON,* Debbie Baker, Pam Buchanan, Karla Flambert, Roger Flambert (Design), Stella Flambert, Vicky Flambert, Pat Grinter, Kathleen Henderson, Azalea Mayhew (Design), George McLaughlin, Wendy McLaughlin, Sany Odone, Philip Ray, Arthur Rogers, Mary Rogers , Julie Rustin, Alice Smith, Jill Smith, Jo Turgoose, Gillian Yarde-Leavett (Design).

6. WEYHILL, SHIPTON BELLINGER, TIDWORTH

TIDWORTH, Molly Ayres, Barbara Babman, Mac Baugh, Sybil Baugh, Maureen Dagger, Gladys Fields, Muriel Harris, Eric

Johnson (Design), Alison Lewis, Sylvia Lewis, Aileen Martin, Barbara Oatley, Edward Otway, Sylvia Pearce, Doris Sweeney, Dan Symonds (Design), Marcia Turnbull, Muriel Vickery, Margaret Wadcock, Joan West, Mary Williams; *SHIPTON BELLINGER*, Sue Ball, Maureen Berry, Freda Bowden, Marie Bryan, Annelise Chamberlain, Robert Cooke (Design), Carole Estlick, John Flowers, Rosemary Flowers, Roz Hanson, Sylvia Hart, Heather Herring, Rozanna Herring (Design), Jean Hinde, Antonia Hiscocks, June Jay, Pam Kearley, Ryan Kearley, Jean Mills, Gwen Phillips, Lynn Phillips, Barbara Pottinger(Design), Ellen Reynolds, Linda Reynolds (Design) , Mary Russell, Alison Sperry, Wendy Sperry, Beryl Vickers, Renate Wilson, Val Winfield, Edward Workman, James Workman, Liz Workman, Rebecca Workman; *WEYHILL*, Jean Barrett (Design), Susan Coleman, Marina Colley, Dorothy Elmer.

7. MONXTON, AMPORT, GRATELEY
MONXTON, Douglas Bliss, Bridget Busk, Carol Childs, Pamela Childs, Diana Coldicott, Joan Couper, Judy Crick, Shona Crick, Brenda Gower, Maisie Lock, Winifred Lock, Irene Marver, Meg McConnell (Design), Lucy Munden, Sylvia Potter, Carol Pratt, Heather Pratt, Veronica Rushworth-Lund, Joy Smith; *AMPORT*, Beryl Baglin, Heidi Carre, Sheila Goacher, Maureen Gumn, Catherine Grylls, Marisa Hayhurst, Sheelagh Mathias, Elizabeth Orchard, Robina Orchard (Design), Betty Spurgeon; *GRATELEY*, Maureen Booth, Rhoda Bucknill (Design), Velma Collett (Design), Anne Collier, Lucy Felton, Edna Forsyth, Eileen Jeffries, Anne King, Elizabeth Medley, Heather Popham, Pat Richards, Hilary Seddon, Juanita Sharman, Pattie Tayler, Gwyneth Tierney, Stephanie Wheatley.

8. ABBOTTS ANN, LITTLE ANN
Alan Selby (Design), Jane Simson.

9. GOODWORTH CLATFORD, UPPER CLATFORD, BARTON STACEY
GOODWORTH CLATFORD, Marjorie Eagar, Anne de Nahlik (Design), Claire Russell (Design), Peggy Strange; *UPPER CLATFORD*, Pamela Baker, Peggy Bandy, Pooch Bathurst-Brown, Valerie Combes, Lina Duckworth, Mrs Edwards, Dee Fenton, Mary George, Jennifer Greenwood, Edith Hunt, Rosemary Johnson-Ferguson, Sylvia Kennedy, Judy Marr, Patricia Mason, Geraldine McCaulder (Design), Patricia Simmonds, Rosemary Walker, Barbara Walter; *BARTON STACEY*, Patricia Coleman, Monica Austin, Gillian Beresford, Jenny Briscoe, Hazel Deacon, Wendy Dewey, Barbara Evans, Audrey Freemantle, Moreen Gifford-Hull, Shane Hearn, Julia Hebden, Elver Jackson, Helen James, Susan Lawton, Helen Litton, Julia Mason, Mavis May, Cheryl McCracken, Sally

Merrison, Jean Mills, Margaret Morris, Anna Peebles, Gordon Piper, William Powell, Vera Riggs, Holly Sambell, Jan Sambell (Design), Ann Scoates, Kelly Scoates, Sarah Scoates, June Stacey, Marilyn Stevens , Jean Talbot, Sandy Thornton, Inja Wainwright, Catherine Wilkinson.

10. CHILBOLTON, WHERWELL, LONGPARISH
CHILBOLTON, Mavil Arnold, Frances Batchelor, Michael Batchelor, Lizzie Batchelor, Sue Batchelor (Design), Thomas Batchelor, Ann Blythe, Madeleine Farrand, June Hayman Joyce, Peter Le Breton, Jean Stephens, Jennie Stobart, Edith Vincent, Pupils of Wherwell Primary School, Members of Chilbolton W.I.; *WHERWELL*, Evelyn Violet Hopkins (Design); *LONGPARISH*, Margaret Barber, Sue Elford, Nancy Goodwin, Sarah Harris , Kathleen Hewlett, Jane Jackson, Margaret Johnson, Kathleen North, Anne Russum, Ella Scott, Mary Snow (Design), Dick Snow, Jane Snow, Peggy Snow, Sue Stevens, Rosemary Tennant, Cecil White, Joy White.

11. THE WALLOPS
NETHER WALLOP, June Anderson, Jane Blaxter, Pat Brown, Joyce Blanchard, Mary Butler Stoney, Anne Burkett, Sheila Dickson, Doug Dickson, Sheila Eyre, Christine Fell, Jackie Fenn, Pat Foot, Jane Gardiner, Fiona Gardiner, Jocelyn Gumn, Kit Harper, Catherine Henderson, Antonia Henderson, Camilla Henderson, Venitia Henderson, Rosemary Jepson Turner, Alma Mouland, Sheila Mouland, Susan Osmond, Anthea Russell, Linda Sherwood, Ellen Smith, Jackie Walker, Phyllis Weeks, Margaret Williams (Design); *OVER WALLOP*, Nancy Franks, Jane Gardiner, Marion Gleadow, Catherine Henderson, Antonia Henderson, Camilla Henderson, Venitia Henderson, Mrs Holton, Jeanette Kinch, Jill Lovett, Mary Rayner, Elizabeth Silcock, Mrs Willey, Margaret Williams (Design).

12. BOROUGH MAP WITH STOCKBRIDGE, LONGSTOCK, LECKFORD
STOCKBRIDGE, LONGSTOCK, LECKFORD, Connie Alderman, Margery Andrews, Barbara Belcher, Marina Bulpitt, Penny Burnfield, Lillian Carrey, Gillian Clark, Lucy Clark, Melaine Clark, Edna Clarke, Pamela Clarke, Kay Clayton, Ena Croker, Dorothy Darby, Rose East, Carolyn Evans, Kate Gibbons, Shirley Guard, Monica Harding, Iris Harman, Rosalind Hill, Sue Hofman, Margaret Humber, Jean Johnson, Elfie Kerrison, Mary Lock , Anne Merridale, Mrs Monaghan, Anne Musters, Mabel Nelmes, Joyce Pye Smith, Betty Rawlence (Design), Dorothy Richardson, Mary Saunders, Barbara Shearwood, Dame Nancy Snagge, Margery Stares, Nina VanGalen, Gladys Wearing, Pauline Webster; *TEST VALLEY BOROUGH MAP*, Lucy Felton, Sheelagh Mathias, Robina Orchard (Design).

13. HOUGHTON, BOSSINGTON AND BROUGHTON
HOUGHTON & BOSSINGTON, Georgia Burgess, Sophie Busk, Pat Cannings, Joan Chant, Margaret Carter, Ann Fairey, Terence and Dorothea FitzGibbon (Design), Esme Fellows, Jill Harding, David Howe, Carol Norton, Lyn Snellgrove, Mary Underwood; *BROUGHTON*, Veronica Chubb, Margot Dent, Elsa Drew, Terence and Dorothea FitzGibbon (Design), David Howe, Joyce Monk, Kathleen Palmer, Diana Puckle, Susan Turpin, Susan Joyce.

14. KING'S SOMBORNE, LITTLE SOMBORNE, UP SOMBORNE, ASHLEY
Davina Adams, Barbara Allan, Louise Andrews, Jeremy Aucock, Kristy Aucock, Linda Aucock, Jenny Baker, Vic Baker, Samantha Baker, Theresse Baker, Audrey Baker, Janet Baker, Muriel Bailey, Prue Barlow, Barbara Barnes, Jaqueline Barnes, James Barry, Audrie Bendall (Design), Frank Bendall, Lily Biddlecombe, Movita Bird, Pat Bird, Eddie Black, Barry Blackmore, Lisa Blackmore, Margery Blake, Kate Broadbridge, Barbara Broadbridge, Anthony Brooke-Webb, Joyce Brooke-Webb, Susannah Brooke-Webb, Simon Brooke-Webb, Tim Brooke-Webb, Joan Brown, Win Brown, Anne Burrell, David Burrell, Vera Burt, Philip Burt, Valerie Burton, Dorothy Butcher, Susan Byrne, Robin Cardwell, Rosemary Cardwell, Ann Carr, Jackie Chalcraft, Elsie Chapman, Phyl Chapman, Anne Clay, Ernie Clay, Henry Cole, Bridget Coleman, Penny Coleman, Loretta Collier, Vivien Clowes, Susan Cripps, Charlotte Cripps, Jean Cummings, Joan Dowty, Geoff Drinkwater, Mary Dutnall, Mike Dutnall, Penny Dyke, James Ede, Sarah Ede, Genette Edwards, Rachel Ewence, Nora Evans, Denise Evans, Diana Eubank-Scott, Lynsay Eubank-Scott, Jessica Eubank-Scott, Andrew Flanaghan, Sheila Fletcher, Bill Fletcher, Phyllis Gardner, Natasha Geary, Steven Geary, Angela Gentry, Harriet Gentry, Richard Gentry, Sarah George, Hannah George, Ivy Gibbons, Jessie Grace, Pat Grieveson, Amy Green, Ann Karin Gunnarson, Mollie Haines, Rita Harfield, Julia Hawkswood, Caroline Hervey-Bathurst, Catherine Henderson, Gillian Hilton, Paul Hilton, Alexander Hilton, Katherine Hilton, Olive Hoare, Ralph Hone, Sybil Hone, Ann Marie Hook, Rosemary Horsey, Margaret Howard, Paul Hurst, Sue Jackson, Alex James, Vera Jones, Claire Jones, Chrissie Johnstone, Tamila Johnstone, Berin Johnstone, Sylvia Kay, Sarah Keeley, Delia King, David King, Lesley King, Stephen King, Jane King, Donna Lane, Jean Lane, Dale Lane, Lily Lane, Lilian Light, Connie Machin, Pat Mahoney, Edna Mackenzie, Patricia Mackenzie, Ann Mackenzie, Anna McCay, Nola McIntosh, Judy McPhee, Sarah McPhee, Nick McPhee, Freda Marchant, Richard Martin, Susan Martin, Terence Martin, Jeanne Mills, Pam Monk, Patricia Newell, Hedley Newell, Cathy Newell, Rowland Newell, Angela O'Leary, Archie O'Leary, Emma O'Leary, Lisa O'Leary, Sian O'Leary, Shane O'Leary, Millie Oram, Denise Orange, Ethel

Osborne, Helen Pearson, Janet Pearson, Gordon Pearson, David Pearson, Chris Pearson, Andrew Peel, Amanda Peel, Mary Perry, Irene Pigott, Cyril Pigott, Nigel Potter, Muriel Potter, Richard Potter, William Potter, Jane Purdue, Betty Ray, Eve Read, Mary Rebbeck, Paul Reynolds, Marjorie Richardson, Janice Robbins, Kevin Robbins, Kerry Robbins, Ellen Rumbold, Sharon Rumbold, Mary Rustell, Bill Saltmarsh, Phyllis Saltmarsh, Kate Saunders, Phil Saunders, Ruth Shepard, Daphne Shotton, Pat Sillence, Lorna Simms, Rosa Sims, Mike Simms, Syd Skinner, Pamela Skinner, June Smith, Les Smith, Adam Spurling, Sue Spurling, Robert Spurling, Ian Stewart, Laura Stewart, Arden Stewart, Kevin Stubbs, Jennifer Stubbs, Joanna Stubbs, Benjamin Stubbs, Amy Swatton, Simon Taylor, Audrey Thomas, Sheila Tickner, Kevin Tickner, Margie Till, Claire Tongs, Mary Turner, Simon Turner, John Vanderpump, Lucy Vanderpump, Joan Verrier, Muriel Way, Leslie Way, Caroline Weeks, Sharron Whatley, Pamela Whatley, Andrea Whatley, Iris Whatley, Nicky Witcher, Mike Woodcock, Kenneth Woolfit, Ian Wilson, Sally Wilson, Jeannie Wilson, Robert Wilson,   Staff and pupils of King's Somborne Primary School,   Hannah Amos, Lynn Amos, Simon Amos, Kieron Andrews, James Aucock, Kirsty Aucock, Dean Baker, Lorna Baker, Michael Baker, Tanya Baker, Claire Baldwin, Jennifer Bamford, Enid Bevan, Aurelie Bevan, Wayne Black, Lisa Blackmore, Helen Bolderstone, Nicola Boyce, Claire Broome, Nicola Bunch, Paul Burrell, Jonathan Cardwell, Thomas Cardwell, Emma Carruthers, Gary Carruthers, Samantha Carruthers, Olive Coates, Amy Coultas, Paul Down, Simon Down, Kevin Downing, Emma Dyke, Caroline Eales, Mark Edwards, Peter Edwards, Mark Evans, Tammy Ewence, Danny Foyle, Natasha Geary, Bernard Grant, Barry Grievson, Wendy Hood, Deborah Howard, Jean Howard, Robert Jackson, Samuel Jackson, Debra Keeley, Geoffrey King, Donna Knights, Charlene Lane, Paul Lane, Max Langton-Lockton, Tabitha Langton-Lockton, Natalie Muggeridge, Wayne Nelmes, David Newell, Sarah Newell, Sian O'Leary, Ashley Oram, David Portsmouth , Jessica Portsmouth, Michael Quick, Emma Rioldi, David Roberts, Victoria Roberts, Thomas Robison, Julie Ross, Debby Sacree, Anita Selman, Lucy Sherred, Emma Snellgrove, Laura Snellgrove, Gary Tickner, Stephen Tickner, Marcus Tongs, Joyce Trueman, Fiona Turner, Richard Verrier, Janice Waterman, Justyn Waterman, Kelly Westbrook, Angela Worgan, Lee Young.

15. MOTTISFONT, NURSLING AND ROWNHAMS, EAST TYTHERLEY
MOTTISFONT, Margery Abraham, Madeleine Aylward, Sylvia Blake, Anne Cameron, Doris Cannons, Barbara Cavanagh, Catherine Cavanagh, Olivia Cavanagh, Susan Clutterbuck, Rachel Fowler, Cythia Fletcher, Canon David Howe, Moira Hulugalle, Edna Mathews, Victoria Muers-Raby, Dolly Newell, Sylvia Pankhurst, Theresa Port, Margaret Spreadbury, Barbara-

Anne Thomas, Joan Thompson, Valda White, Cathy Wood, Gordon Wood (Design); *NURSLING AND ROWNHAMS,* Barbara Dawe, Christopher Kemp, Lin Kemp (Design), Judith Lawry, Bunny Mann, Leslie Mann, Mildred McGroarty; *EAST TYTHERLEY,* Margaret Downe, Ina Redshaw, Pamela Russell, Joyce Sowden, Marjorie West (Design).

16. MICHELMERSH, BRAISHFIELD, LOCKERLEY
MICHELMERSH, Joyce Brown, Celia Cox, Mary Lees, Shirley Morrish (Design), Eileen Newcomb, Vanessa Pink, Shirley Price, Elizabeth Webb, Betty Welch; *BRAISHFIELD,* Joyce Alford, Margaret Batchelor, Barbara Bell, Sarah Boothman, Millie Dunford, Elizabeth Ellison, Evelyn Eustace, Jose Fare, Olive Fuller, Esme Kidd, Marilyn Madigan (Design), Enid Oliver, Ruby Payn, Margery Penton, Patricia Roe, Diana Selka, Elizabeth Sheppard, Magdalen Sleeman, Ms E Stuart-Smith, Jill Van-Rooijen, Freda Vrotsos, Head Master and pupils of Braishfield Primary School, Katie Appleton, Stuart Bakewell, Alexia Bell, Thomas Bird, Charlotte Butterfield, Lucy Butterfield, Stuart Chalder, Beverley Corrigan, Robin Corrigan, Hannah Cross, Daniella Dejonge, Koos Dejonge, Tom Dejonge, Jonathan Forch, Josh Hampton, Andrew Hansom, Jonathan Haysom, Darren Hayter, Ashley Herridge, Biba Herridge, Emily Hobday, Alex Hodgson, Damian Howkins, Lucy Howkins, Fiona Hunt, Guy Hunt, Oliver Johnson, Richard King, Ruth King, Luke Kington, Mark Krey, James Lanham, Nicholas Lawson, Caroline Leach, Ben Leatherdale, Luke Leatherdale, Rowena Lewis, Vicky Lewis, James Light, Joanne Light, Darren Manton, Neil McKay, Morris Miles, Darrel Milsom, Richard Milsom, Colin Morris, Hayley Morris, Rachael Morris, Sarah Musslewhite, Lorraine Norman, Ryan Norman, Michael Passe, Sharron Passe, Lee Payne, Matthew Payne, Ewen Ross, Andrew Scott, Peter Scott, Christopher Spacagna, Jenny Spacagna, Ralph Stevens, David Thomas, Stacey Tiley, Brett Turner, Anna Vrotsos, Sebastian West, Tristan West, Phillip Wildman, Cally Wilkinson, Jenna Wilkinson, Timothy Wordsworth; *LOCKERLEY,* Olwen Allen, Betty Anning, Joyce Bullock, Peter Bullock, Frederick Courtney OBE, Marion Courtney (Design), Jo Earwood, Dolores Ford, Diana McMillan, Margaret Niblett, Mollie Parsons, Isabel Stileman, Margaret Williams.

17. AWBRIDGE, SHERFIELD ENGLISH, WELLOW
AWBRIDGE, Doreen Bethell (Design), Ann Goulden, Pauline Harris, Pam Hillier, Margaret Hutchens, Anne Jones, Rosemary Oakeshott, Joy Skinner, Liz Stringer; *SHERFIELD ENGLISH,* Lilian Biddlecombe, Tessa East, Myra Galton, Margaret George, Ursula Goodyear, Fay Heath (Design), Shirley Lemon, Barbara Sharp, Elisabeth Smith; *WELLOW,* Valerie Braithwaite, Marjorie Dorling (Design), Kathleen Eburn, Maureen Harris, Jean Watkins, Joyce Weberstadt, Psyche Veall.

18. ROMSEY, ROMSEY EXTRA
Mary Akerman, Madeleine Aylward, Marie Bailey, Margaret Barber, Phoebe Bartleet, Iris Bradstock, Jan Brown, Pat Caldwell, Florence Clubley, Sara Credland, Joan Darlingon, Violet Delves, Joyce Downer, Thelma Dowling, Joan Duley, Elizabeth Ford-Smith, Caroline Gardiner, Olive Grant, Dora Grieves, Bib Hale, Doreen Hedger, Joy Hendley, Patti Johnson, Annette Jones (Design), Janet Knowles, Yvonne Matcham, Jan Middleton, Sara Moore, Phyllis Newman, Pam Palmer, R Pennells, Elizabeth Pickard, Stephanie Powell, Nan Ramsden, Betty Salter, Eileen Seaman, Mary Seaman, Carole Smith, Mary Thornton, June Thorpe, Chris Turton, Evelyn Wardingley, Nancy Wells, Grace White, Barbara Whittle.

19. NORTH BADDESLEY, AMPFIELD, CHILWORTH
NORTH BADDESLEY, Clothilde Bulling, Cas Hamilton, Pam Morecraft, Doreen Parker (Design), Geoff Pretty (Design) , Eileen Siers, Doris Stapleford, Lilian Thomason (Design) , Jean Trundle (Design); *AMPFIELD,* Phyllis Harris (Design), Pupils of Ampfield C.E.Primary School, Luke Andrews, Simon Andrews, Chloe Anthias, Penelope Anthias, Robert Birkett, Alison Brett, Thomas Burden, Neil Chapman, Matthew Clancy, Paul Day, Christopher Drew, Timothy Evans, Caroline Everden, Roland Fowler, Samantha Garner, Maria Gratton, Alexandra Gray, Jennifer Langridge, Matthew Langridge, Joanna Lawes, Sarah Lawes, Helen Oldham, Alexander Ralph, Simon Rusher, Natasha Scarrott, Carley Stephens, Matthew Storey,   Members of Ampfield Women's Institute, Members of Ampfield Parish Council, Members of Ampfield "Get Together Club", Members of St Mark's Craft Group; *CHILWORTH,* Glenna Burdsall, Pat Cameron, Jean Hudson, Joan Mears, Betty Mobbs, Betsy Lester, Shelia Robinson, Frank Stokes (Design), Janet Stokes, Moira O'Malley, Norah Wynne.

Note: *The details and names of contributors recorded above were provided by representatives of each tapestry group.*

Printed by BAS Printers Ltd, Over Wallop, Stockbridge, Hampshire